sewNEWS

the trusted sewing source

P UT A LITTLE bit of personality in everything you sew by learning simple embellishments that take projects from pretty to spectacular. Make your own fabric by stamping; add sparkle with grommets and eyelets; layer ruffles in unique ways; felt fabulous designs into fiber; and more! The possibilities are endless with a little inspiration offered in the pages of this book. Accent your home, bling out your accessories and adorn your garments effortlessly with the expert tips, tricks and techniques that follow.

For more information,
visit **sewnews.com.**

LEISURE ARTS
the art of everyday living
www.leisurearts.com

sewNEWS
741 Corporate Circle, Ste. A
Golden, CO, 80401
sewnews.com

SEW NEWS STAFF
Editorial
Editor-in-Chief: Ellen March
Senior Editor: Beth Bradley
Associate Editor: Nicole LaFoille
Web Editor: Jill Case
Editorial Assistant: Jessica Giardino
Art
Creative Director: Sue Dothage
Graphic Designer: Erin Hershey
Assistant Graphic Designer: Courtney Kraig
Illustrator: Melinda Bylow
Photography: Brent Ward,
Mellisa Karlin Mahoney
Hair & Makeup Stylists: Angela Lewis

CREATIVE CRAFTS GROUP
SVP/General Manager: Tina Battock
SVP/Chief Marketing Officer: Nicole McGuire
VP/Production & Technology: Barbara Schmitz
OPERATIONS
Associate Publisher: Wendy Thompson
Circulation Manager: Deb Westmaas
New Business Manager: Adriana Maldonado
Renewal and Billing Manager: Nekeya Dancy
Digital Marketing Director: Kristen Allen
Digital Marketing Manager: Jodi Lee
Newsstand Consultant: TJ Montilli
Production Manager: Michael J. Rueckwald
Product and Video Development:
Kristi Loeffelholz
Advertising Coordinator: Madalene Becker
Administrative Assistant: Jane Flynn
Retail Sales: LaRita Godfrey: (800) 815-3538

F+W MEDIA INC.
Chairman & CEO: David Nussbaum
CFO & COO: James Ogle
President: Sara Domville
President: David Blansfield
Chief Digital Officer: Chad Phelps
VP/E-Commerce: Lucas Hilbert
Senior VP/Operations: Phil Graham
VP/Communications: Stacie Berger

LEISURE ARTS STAFF
Editorial Staff
Vice President of Editorial: Susan White Sullivan
Creative Art Director: Katherine Laughlin
Publications Director: Leah Lampirez
Special Projects Director: Susan Frantz Wiles
Prepress Technician: Stephanie Johnson

Business Staff
President and Chief Executive Officer:
Rick Barton
Senior Vice President of Operations:
Jim Dittrich
Vice President of Finance: Fred F. Pruss
Vice President of Sales-Retail Books:
Martha Adams
Vice President of Mass Market:
Bob Bewighouse
Vice President of Technology and Planning:
Laticia Mull Dittrich
Controller: Tiffany P. Childers
Information Technology Director: Brian Roden
Director of E-Commerce: Mark Hawkins
Manager of E-Commerce: Robert Young
Retail Customer Service Manager: Stan Raynor

Library of Congress Control Number: 2014934757
ISBN-13/EAN: 978-1-4647-1545-7
UPC: 0-28906-06313-4

contents

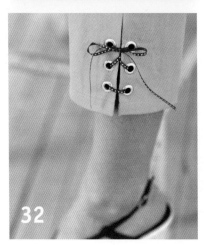

58

54

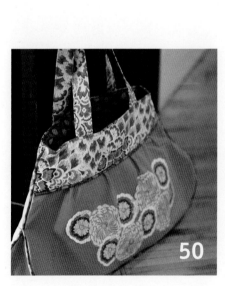

50

61

16

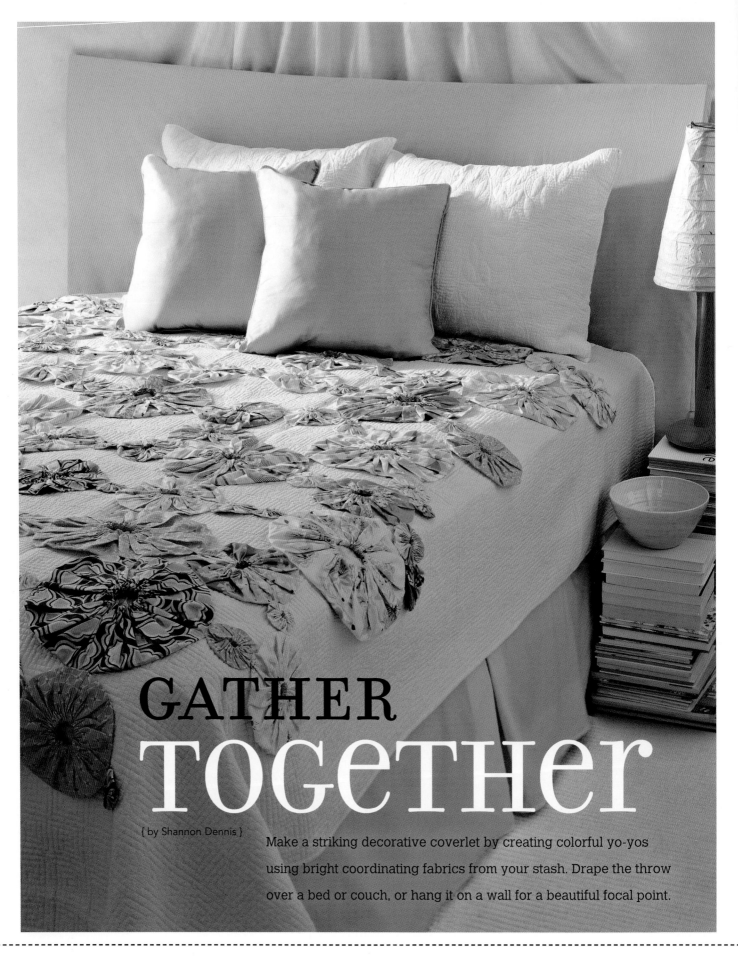

GATHER
TOGETHER

{ by Shannon Dennis }

Make a striking decorative coverlet by creating colorful yo-yos using bright coordinating fabrics from your stash. Drape the throw over a bed or couch, or hang it on a wall for a beautiful focal point.

Supplies

- **12 coordinating cotton fabrics** (amount determined by yardage chart)
- **All-purpose thread**
- **Hand sewing needle**
- **Removable fabric marker**

Yardage Chart		
Twin	Full/Queen	King
1.5 yards	3 yards	3.5 yards

Cut

TWIN
From the 12 coordinating fabrics, cut eighteen 4″-diameter circles, twenty-seven 6″-diameter circles, eighteen 9″-diameter circles, twenty-seven 13″-diameter circles and twenty-seven 20″-diameter circles.

FULL/QUEEN
From the 12 coordinating fabrics, cut thirty-six 4″-diameter circles, fifty-four 6″-diameter circles, thirty-six 9″-diameter circles, fifty-four 13″-diameter circles and fifty-four 20″-diameter circles.

KING
From the 12 coordinating fabrics, cut forty-five 4″-diameter circles, sixty-eight 6″-diameter circles, forty-five 9″-diameter circles, sixty-eight 13″-diameter circles and sixty-eight 20″-diameter circles.

Yo-Yos
Fold one circle outer edge ¼″ toward the wrong side; press. Thread a hand sewing needle with all-purpose thread; knot the end. Stitch a running stitch around the circle perimeter, closely following the folded edge. Leave a long thread tail **(1)**.

Gently pull the thread tail, gathering the circle center **(2)**. Evenly distribute the gathers, if necessary. Take one last stitch, and then knot the thread end close to the yo-yo to secure. Press the yo-yo flat.

Repeat to create yo-yos from the remaining circles.

Construct
Use ¼″ seam allowances unless otherwise noted.

For the twin size, position 10 to 13 yo-yos on a flat work surface to create one 75″-long row. For the full/queen or king size, position

Tip: Learn more about making yo-yos on page 7.

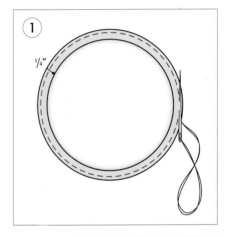

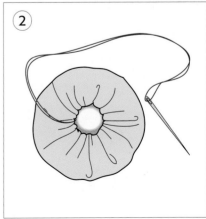

Tip: Use fabric scraps to make each yo-yo. Contrasting prints add to the charm.

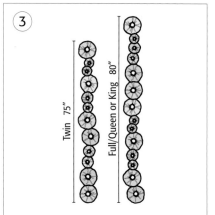

③

Twin 75"

Full/Queen or King 80"

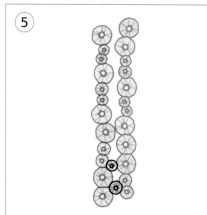

⑤

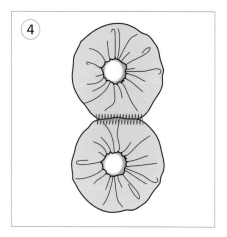

④

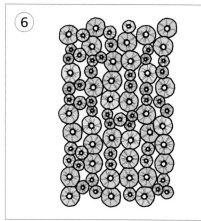

⑥

as many yo-yos as necessary to create one 80″-long row (3).

Repeat to make nine rows for the twin size, 18 rows for the full/queen size and 23 rows for the king size.

Select a zigzag stitch on the machine. Abut two yo-yos, and then stitch, catching both yo-yo edges in the stitching. Stitch over the same stitching line several times to secure (4). Continue stitching the remaining yo-yos to create the first row.

Abut the first row lower edge and second row upper edge. Using a zigzag stitch, tack the yo-yos at each intersection.

Fill in large spaces by incorporating extra yo-yos, if necessary (5). Repeat to attach the remaining rows.

For a unique look, stagger the rows so the edges aren't perfectly aligned (6). ✂

SOURCE
Free Spirit Fabrics provided Heather Bailey's Nicey Jane fabric: (866) 907-3305, freespiritfabric.com.

BASIC SKILLS:
YO-YOS

{ by Lucy Blaire }

Yo-yos are a perfect way to use up small fabric scraps and create exciting embellishments. Learn about different yo-yo types, and then choose from three projects to feature the trendy technique.

History

Fabric yo-yos were popular in the '20s and '30s and were most likely inspired by the popular toy with the same name. They became a widespread trend because women could easily carry small fabric scraps with them to create yo-yos.

Yo-Yo Maker

Many companies manufacture fabric yo-yo makers in a variety of design shapes, such as round, flower and butterfly. A traditional yo-yo maker contains a round plastic disk with a ridged perimeter and a tray with a notched perimeter as a stitching guide.

Cut a fabric shape ½″ larger than the tray perimeter. Center the fabric right side down over the tray. Center

Tip: To draw perfect circle templates, divide the desired yo-yo diameter in half; record as the radius. Using a compass and ruler, spread the compass legs to equal the radius, and then draw the circle; cut out.

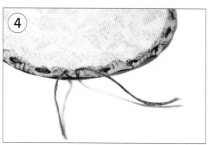

the disk over the fabric, and then snap the disk into the tray, sandwiching the fabric between the tray and disk. Trim the excess fabric to a ¼" seam allowance **(1)**.

Thread a hand sewing needle with a length of thread or embroidery floss; knot the end. Bring the needle up through one tray notch, and then push the needle down through the adjacent notch, catching the seam allowance in the stitching. Repeat to stitch the entire disk perimeter.

Trim the thread, leaving long thread tails. Remove the disk from the tray and the fabric from the disk **(2)**.

Follow the finishing instructions on page 9 to finish the desired yo-yo type.

Templates

Creating a yo-yo using a template instead of a maker is slightly more work, but the results are the same.

From card stock, cut one 4¾"-diameter and one 5¼"-diameter circle to create a 1¾"-diameter round yo-yo. Proportionally increase or decrease the diameters to create different yo-yo sizes.

Using the large template, cut one fabric circle. Center the small template on the fabric circle wrong side. Press the fabric edges around the circle template using an iron on a medium setting without steam **(3)**.

Carefully remove the small template from the fabric circle. Thread a hand sewing needle with a length of thread or embroidery floss; knot the end. Stitch a ¼"-long running stitch along the circle pressed edge, beginning

and ending the stitching on the fabric wrong side **(4)**.

Follow the finishing instructions on page 9 to finish the desired yo-yo type.

Yo-Yo Types

TRADITIONAL: Traditional yo-yos are attached to another fabric as embellishment.

To create a traditional yo-yo, prepare a yo-yo according to the chosen method. Gently pull the thread tails to tightly gather the fabric, making sure the gathers are centered. Double knot the thread tails to secure, and then trim the ends **(5)**. Use a pin to evenly distribute the gathers and push the knot toward the fabric wrong side.

STAND ALONE: Stand-alone yo-yos aren't attached to another fabric. Create flat or pillowed yo-yos to embellish a variety of projects. Stitch together stand-alone yo-yos for a 3-D quilt or use them individually for decorations, such as the "Bag Clip" project on page 10.

To create a flat stand-alone yo-yo, construct a yo-yo following the traditional yo-yo instructions, but don't attach it to another fabric.

To create a pillowed stand alone yo-yo, prepare a yo-yo according to the chosen method. Gently pull the thread tails to slightly gather the fabric. Loosely stuff the yo-yo with fiberfill, and then completely gather the yo-yo. Double knot the thread tails, and then trim the ends. Use a pin to evenly distribute the gathers and push the knot toward the fabric wrong side **(6)**.

TRADITIONAL APPLIQUÉ: Stitch traditional appliqué yo-yos directly onto backing fabric to embellish bags, quilts or clothing.

To create a traditional appliqué yo-yo, prepare a yo-yo according to the chosen method.

From card stock, cut one stitching template circle between ¹⁄₃ and ¹⁄₂ smaller than a yo-yo maker tray or large template (depending on the desired finished diameter).

Place the yo-yo fabric wrong side up on a flat work surface. Center the stitching template over the yo-yo wrong side; trace the template perimeter. With right sides together, place the yo-yo over the chosen backing fabric or garment. Machine stitch the yo-yo to the backing fabric or garment following the stitching line **(7).**

Gently pull the thread tails to tightly gather the yo-yo fabric circle, centering the gathers. Double knot the thread tails, and then trim the ends. Use a pin to evenly distribute the gathers and push the knot toward the fabric wrong side **(8).**

OPEN APPLIQUÉ: An open appliqué yo-yo is the same as a traditional appliqué yo-yo except the stitching template diameter is increased, which prevents the gathers from completely closing, leaving the yo-yo fabric wrong side exposed.

To create an open appliqué yo-yo, prepare a yo-yo according to the chosen method.

From card stock, cut one stitching template circle ⁵⁄₈ smaller than a yo-yo maker tray or large template.

Place the yo-yo wrong side up on a flat work surface. Center the stitching template over the yo-yo wrong side;

trace the template perimeter. With right sides together, place the yo-yo over the chosen backing fabric or garment. Machine stitch the yo-yo to the backing fabric or garment along the stitching line **(9).**

Gently pull the thread tails to tightly gather the fabric circle, centering the gathers. Double knot the thread tails, and then trim the ends. Use a pin to evenly distribute the gathers and push the knot toward the fabric wrong side **(10).**

To tack the yo-yo gathered edge to the backing fabric, thread a hand sewing needle with a length of thread or embroidery floss; knot the end. Beginning at the backing fabric wrong side, bring the needle up through the backing fabric and catch two or three thread strands from one yo-yo gathered edge. Push the needle through the backing fabric underneath the first stitch, and then pull tight. Repeat to stitch every gather that touches the backing fabric. When complete, knot the thread on the backing fabric wrong side and trim the thread ends. Remove the yo-yo gathering stitch. Adjust the gathers to create an even ruffled texture.

OPEN APPLIQUÉ WITH INSET: An open appliqué yo-yo with inset is the same as an open appliqué yo-yo except

Tip: Use lightweight cottons, such as quilting weight, when making yo-yos. Thicker fabrics look stiff and bulky when gathered.

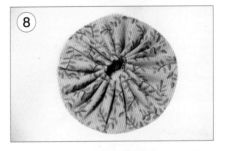

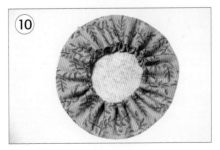

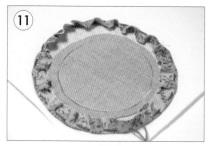

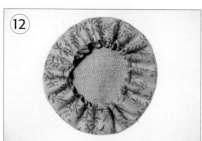

a coordinating fabric piece is stitched on the yo-yo fabric wrong side.

To create an open appliqué yo-yo, prepare a yo-yo according to the chosen method.

From card stock, cut one stitching template circle ⁵/₈ smaller than a yo-yo maker tray or large template. Trace the stitching template on coordinating fabric, and then cut out the circle ¹/₄″ beyond the stitching line.

Place the yo-yo wrong side up on a flat work surface. Center the inset fabric over the yo-yo wrong side.

With right sides together, place the yo-yo over the chosen backing fabric or garment. Machine stitch the yo-yo and inset fabric to the backing fabric or garment along the stitching line (11).

Gently pull the thread tails to tightly gather the yo-yo, centering the gathers. Double knot the thread tails, and then trim the ends. Use a pin to evenly distribute the gathers and push the knot toward the fabric wrong side (12).

Follow the tacking instructions on page 9 to hand stitch the gathered edge to the fabric.

OFFSET APPLIQUÉ YO-YO WITH INSET: Offset appliqué yo-yos have an asymmetrical yo-yo center, creating an unexpected and fun look.

To create an offset appliqué yo-yo with inset, prepare a yo-yo according to the chosen method.

From card stock, cut one offset template circle ¹/₂ smaller than a yo-yo maker tray or large template. Trace the offset template on coordinating fabric, and then cut out the circle ¹/₄″ beyond the stitching line.

Place the yo-yo wrong side up on a flat work surface. Place the inset fabric wrong side over the yo-yo fabric wrong side, offsetting it to one side. With right sides together, place the yo-yo over the chosen backing fabric or garment. Machine stitch the yo-yo and inset fabric to the backing fabric or garment along the stitching line (13).

Gently pull the thread tails to tightly gather the fabric circle, centering the gathers over the inset. Double knot the thread tails, and then trim the ends. Use a pin to evenly distribute the gathers and push the knot toward the fabric wrong side (14).

Follow the tacking instructions on page 9 to hand stitch the gathered edge to the fabric.

Bag Clip

Let stand-alone yo-yos shine with fun clips to personalize and decorate favor bags at your next party.

Supplies

- **Assorted print cotton fabrics (amount according to desired size and number of yo-yos)**
- **Clothespins & party favor bags (amount according to the number of yo-yos)**
- **All-purpose thread**
- **Embroidery floss**
- **Card stock**
- **Hand embroidery needle**

Prepare

Using the flag template on page 63, trace the desired number of flags onto card stock; cut out. Write the name of each party guest onto the flags at least 1″ from the short end.

Construct

Create the desired number of flat stand-alone yo-yos following the instructions on page 8.

Thread a hand embroidery needle with a length of embroidery floss; knot the end. Center one yo-yo wrong side over one flag short end right side.

Hand stitch the yo-yo and flag together, making sure to only catch the yo-yo fabric wrong side. Loop the thread around one clothespin clamp twice near the hinge lower edge, and then take two more stitches through the flag and yo-yo. Knot the thread along the clothespin clamp; trim the ends (A).

Use your fingers to lightly curl the flag and distribute the yo-yo gathers. Clip to the party favor bag.

Repeat to create the desired number of clips.

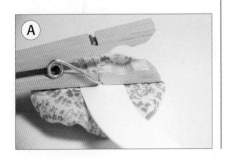

Chair Cushion

Use pillowed yo-yos to create a comfy chair cushion.

Supplies

Supplies listed are enough to make one 13"x15" cushion.

- 6 coordinating print cotton fat quarters
- Two 2"x10" print cotton strips
- Two ¼"x2" adhesive hook-and-loop rectangles
- All-purpose thread
- Embroidery floss
- Fiberfill
- Hand embroidery needle

Construct

Create fifty-six 1³/₄"-diameter pillowed yo-yos from six coordinating print cotton fabrics, following the instructions on page 8.

On a flat work surface, place the pillowed yo-yos in seven rows of eight yo-yos.

Thread a hand embroidery needle with a length of embroidery floss; knot the end. With right sides together, align two adjacent yo-yo edges from the first row; whipstitch using a ½"-long tacking stitch (B). Repeat to stitch each yo-yo row, and then stitch each row together.

Place the seat cushion on the chair and pin-mark the yo-yos that touch the chair back.

Fold each strip in half lengthwise with wrong sides together; unfold. Fold each short end ½" toward the wrong side; press. Fold each long edge toward the center foldline; press. Edgestitch the long and short open edges. Designate a right and wrong side.

Adhere the hook rectangle along one strip short end wrong side. Adhere the loop rectangle along the opposite strip short end right side (C). Repeat to create the remaining strap.

Fold each strip in half widthwise; pin-mark the center. Pin each strip center to the cushion pin-mark; hand stitch. ✂

SOURCE
Clover Needlecraft carries yo-yo makers in a variety of shapes: (800) 233-1703, clover-usa.com.

COLORFUL COLLaGE

{ by Linda MacPhee }

Free-motion stitching allows you to draw unique artistic designs with thread. This technique is a fun and easy way to embellish and customize fabric for garments, quilts and home décor. Learn the keys to successful free-motion stitching and put your skills to work to decorate a one-of-a-kind jacket.

MacPhee Workshop
#35 Blazer Bonanza

Free-Motion Notions

Free-motion stitching is enabled when the sewing machine feed dogs are disengaged and the presser foot hovers over the throat plate. When engaged, the feed dogs guide the fabric toward the machine back, but when they're lowered, it's possible to stitch in any direction. Refer to the machine manual for instructions on how to lower the feed dogs.

A specialty free-motion or darning presser foot helps control the fabric and allows you to see the stitches as you sew. Contact your machine dealer or manufacturer to find a free-motion foot suitable for your machine make and model.

For best results when incorporating this technique on a garment, select an uncomplicated pattern with minimal seams. Use a firm, stable fabric, such as cotton twill or flannel-backed satin. These fabrics are resistant to slipping and puckering during stitching. For extra security and to maintain tautness, hoop the fabric area when free-motion stitching. Any thread type is suitable for free-motion stitching, but for more contrast, use heavyweight rayon thread or decorative metallic thread.

Before beginning a project, test-stitch on fabric scraps. Install the machine's table or flat bed attachment, if applicable, to provide a larger sewing surface. Practice "doodling" by carefully guiding the fabric with both hands. Draw an assortment of lines, curves and squiggles until you're comfortable with the machine speed.

Jazzy Jacket

Supplies

- Sewing machine capable of free-motion stitching
- Jacket pattern (see "Sources.")
- Heavyweight woven fabric and notions (as indicated on pattern envelope)
- Heavyweight rayon embroidery thread
- Assortment of 80 to 100 fabric scraps no larger than 5″ square
- Free-motion or darning foot
- Removable fabric marker
- Fabric glue (such as Glue Pins)

Cut

Choose any desired jacket pattern.

Roughly cut out all of the jacket pattern pieces from the fabric, allowing an additional 1″ border around each pattern piece perimeter. This border enables you to maintain a secure grip on the fabric and allows for possible shrinkage, as the fabric may pucker during stitching.

Cut the fabric scraps into shapes, such as squares, strips, circles and rectangles, as desired.

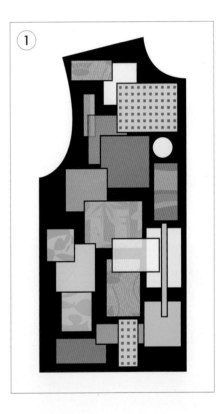

Tip: For extra contrast when free-motion stitching, use a twin needle threaded with contrasting thread colors.

zippers

{ by Lyn Browne, courtesy of Coats & Clark }

EXPOSED

Learn how to insert an exposed zipper into a center-back or side seam to create a fashion-forward shift dress. Complete the look with fun decorative zipper embellishments.

McCall's 6068, View A

Tip: When stitching past the zipper pull, lower the needle into the fabric, lift the foot, and then slightly unzip the zipper. Lower the presser foot and stitch for 2″, and then zip the zipper.

Dress
Supplies

- Dress pattern (such as McCall's 6068)
- Fabric and notions (according to pattern envelope)
- Two 1″ x 17″ strips of lightweight fusible interfacing
- 16″ fashion zipper
- All-purpose thread
- Removable fabric marker
- Zipper foot

Get Started

From the fabric, cut out the dress back pieces. Position one dress back piece right side up on a flat work surface.

Position the zipper lengthwise along the center seamline. Pin-mark the zipper end, and then mark a second line ½″ above the first mark, using a removable fabric marker.

Trim away the seam allowance, ending at the second mark **(1)**.

Position one interfacing strip lengthwise along the dress zipper opening with wrong sides together, extending past the second mark; fuse, following the manufacturer's instructions. Transfer the marks to the interfacing **(2)**. Repeat to interface the remaining dress back piece.

Construct

With right sides together and the zipper closed, align the right zipper tape edge with the right back opening; pin **(3)**.

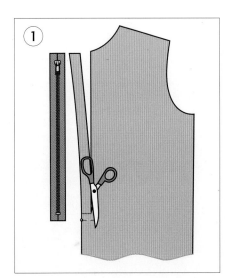

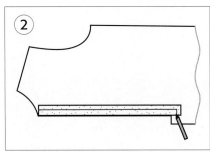

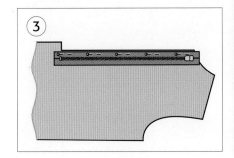

ZIPPER RUFFLE

Add pizzazz to a garment with a simple ruffle made from coordinating zipper tape.

Supplies
- 9″-long closed-bottom zipper
- Heavyweight thread
- Seam sealant
- Zipper foot
- Wire cutters (optional)

Separate the zipper. Cut off the zipper slider end using wire cutters or old scissors. Don't use sharp fabric scissors, as the metal zipper can permanently damage the blades.

Apply seam sealant to the zipper tape ends, following the manufacturer's instructions.

Thread the machine with heavyweight thread in the needle and bobbin. Install a zipper foot.

Stitch ⅛″ from the zipper outer edge, using a long gathering stitch; leave long thread tails.

Knot the thread on one zipper end, and then gently pull the thread on the opposite end to gather. Pull the thread until the zipper tape ruffles; knot the thread ends **(A)**.

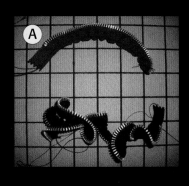

DRESS BIB

Embellish a matching bib necklace with zipper rosettes and ruffles for a fancy look.

Supplies
- Bib pattern
  (such as McCall's 6068, View A)
- 3 zipper rosettes
- 1 long zipper ruffle
- 2 small zipper ruffles
- Heavyweight thread
- Hand sewing needle

CONSTRUCT

Construct the bib necklace, following the pattern guidesheet.

Position the rosettes along the bib lower edge, following the curve and referring to the photo at left. Thread a hand sewing needle with heavyweight thread; stitch each rosette wrong side to the bib.

Position one small ruffle to the right of the rosettes; stitch to the bib. Position the remaining small ruffle to the left of the rosette; stitch to the bib.

Position the long ruffle along the bib left side. Hand stitch the ruffle to the bib.

ZIPPER ROSETTE

Create dimension with simple zipper rosettes.

Supplies
- 24"-long separating zipper
- Heavyweight thread
- Seam sealant
- Pin back
- Hand sewing needle
- Matching felt scrap
- Wire cutters (optional)

Separate the zipper. Cut off the zipper slider end from each zipper using wire cutters or old scissors. Don't use sharp fabric scissors, as the metal zipper can permanently damage the blades.

Apply seam sealant to the zipper tape ends, following the manufacturer's instructions.

Gather the zipper outer edge as for the Zipper Ruffle.

Thread a hand sewing needle with heavyweight thread. Roll one zipper tape end, following the gathering curve to create a rosette. Hand stitch each layer at the center to secure **(A)**. When the rosette is complete, take several stitches across the rosette back to secure.

Cut a small circle of matching felt that's the diameter of the rosette back. Hand stitch the circle to the rosette back.

Stitch a pin back to the rosette back, if desired, to create a separate pin.

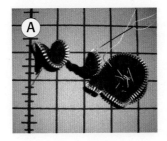

Install a zipper foot. Stitch ¼" from the zipper teeth, ending the stitching at the zipper stop.

With right sides together, align the left zipper-tape edge with the left back opening; pin, and then stitch ¼" from the zipper teeth, ending the stitching at the zipper stop.

Install a standard presser foot onto the machine. Align the dress back pieces with right sides together; pin, and then stitch the center-back seam beginning just below the zipper end mark. Press open the seam.

Clip the seam allowance diagonally toward the stitching end, allowing the seam allowance to lay flat.

Stitch across the zipper tape lower edge and seam allowance through all layers, beginning and ending at the previous stitching lines; press **(4)**.

Finish
Finish constructing the garment, following the pattern guidesheet. ✃

SOURCE
Coats & Clark provided Dual Duty all-purpose thread, Dual Duty XP heavyweight thread and the zippers: (800) 648-1479, coatsandclark.com.

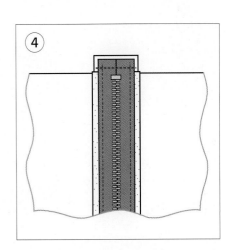

ZIP
TO IT

{ by Cheryl Stranges }

Customize a zippered jacket with decorative trim, chain-stitching and quilting.

Kwik Sew
2896

Supplies

- Jacket pattern (See "Sources.")
- Jacket fabric, notions & separating zipper (according to pattern envelope)
- ½ yard of coordinating batik fabric
- Thread: matching all-purpose, decorative serger & polyester monofilament
- ½ yard of fusible interfacing
- ½ yard of low-loft batting
- Serger (See "Sources.")
- Coordinating netting-style yarn
- Removable fabric marker or chalk

Prepare

Choose any desired jacket pattern with minimal details.

Prewash the fabric to eliminate shrinkage. From the jacket fabric, cut out the sleeves, side-front and back pieces.

From the batik fabric, cut out the collar, facing and front-panel pieces. Cut at least 1" beyond the desired size cutting line to allow for shrinkage after embellishing.

From the batting, cut out the front-panel pieces and one collar.

From the interfacing, cut out the front-panel pieces, facings and one collar.

Fuse the interfacing pieces to the corresponding fabric pieces following the manufacturer's instructions.

Embellish

Mark diagonal parallel quilting lines as desired on the batik front-panel, facing and collar piece right sides. The quilting lines on the featured jacket are spaced approximately 3" apart (1).

Refer to your serger manual to set the serger for chainstitching. Disengage the serger knife and thread the loopers with decorative thread. Test-serge on a batik fabric scrap to determine the necessary tension settings.

Position the fabric left-front panel right side up over the batting left-front panel; pin. Repeat to layer the fabric right-front panel over the batting right-front panel. Layer the fabric upper collar over the batting collar.

Chainstitch the right-front panel along the marked quilting lines through both layers. Repeat to chainstitch the left-front panel and upper collar.

Chainstitch the batik facing pieces and undercollar.

Horizontally stretch the yarn to create a flat netting surface. Position the stretched yarn as desired over the quilted front panels; pin (2).

Thread the machine with monofilament thread. Stitch the yarn long edges.

Trim the batik front-panel and collar edges to fit the original paper pattern pieces.

Construct

Construct the jacket and install the front zipper according to the pattern guidesheet.

If desired, serge-finish the bodice and sleeve lower edges, and then stitch a blind hem using monofilament thread. ✂

SOURCES

Kwik Sew provided the pattern: kwiksew.com.

Husqvarna Viking provided the Designer Diamond Deluxe and Sapphire sewing machines, S 25 Serger, needles and interfacing: (800) 446-2333, husqvarnaviking.com.

Robison Anton provided the decorative serger thread: (800) 847-3235, www.robison-anton.com.

Tip: When combining fabrics of varying weights in one garment, adjust the serger differential feed settings as needed to prevent seam puckering.

Tip: When inserting a separating zipper, substitute washable basting tape for pins to prevent the fabric layers from shifting. Or use basting tape to secure the fabric when stitching a hem.

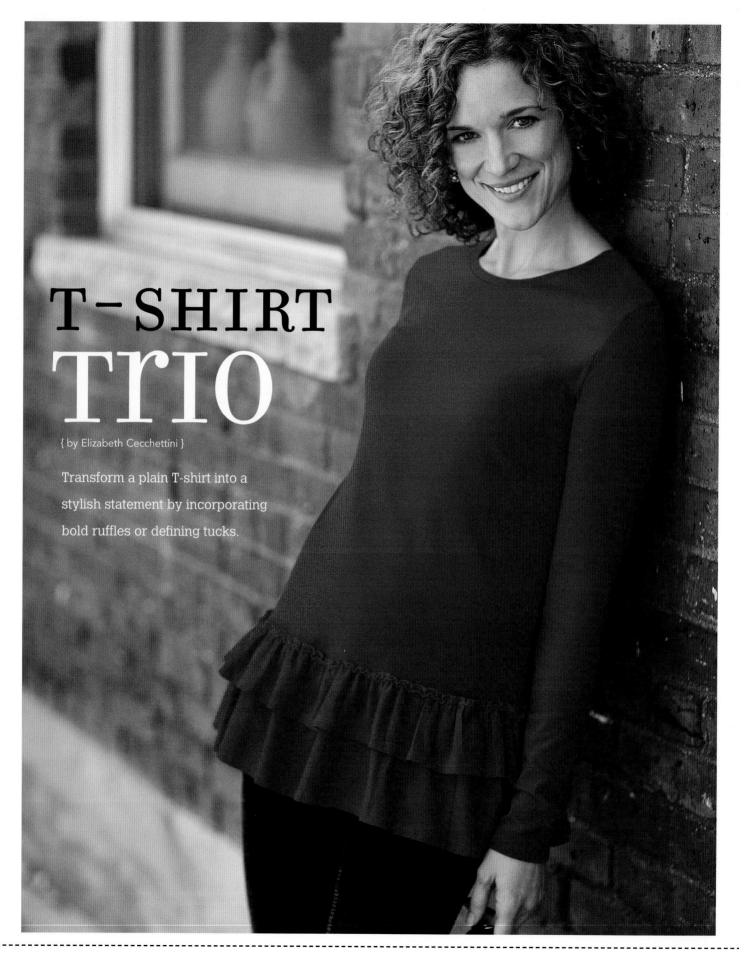

T-SHIRT
Trio

{ by Elizabeth Cecchettini }

Transform a plain T-shirt into a
stylish statement by incorporating
bold ruffles or defining tucks.

Tip: Experiment with contrasting T-shirts or knits to create the ruffles.

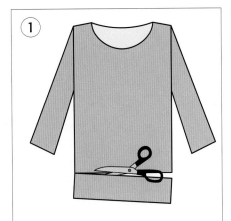

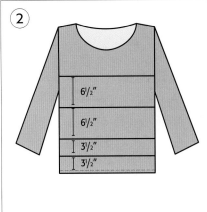

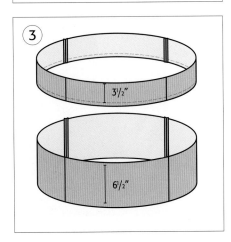

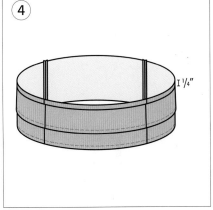

Bottom Ruffle

Supplies

- Long-sleeve T-shirt (fitted)
- Long-sleeve T-shirt
  (2 sizes larger)
- Lightweight tear-away stabilizer
- All-purpose thread
- Removable fabric marker

Prepare

Try on the fitted T-shirt and mark at the hip bones, about 6″ below the natural waist. Remove the T-shirt and position it front side up on a flat work surface. Draw a straight line connecting the hip bone marks, and then cut along the line (1).

Measure the T-shirt raw edge circumference. Double the measurement to obtain the total length needed for each ruffle; record.

Position the larger T-shirt front side up on a flat work surface. Using a removable fabric marker, draw a horizontal line 3½″ from the T-shirt lower edge. Mark a second line 3½″ from the first, a third line 6½″ from the second and a fourth line 6½″ from the third (2).

Cut along the marked lines for the ruffles. Cut open one side seam to create the ruffle strip.

Construct

Use ½″ seam allowances unless otherwise noted.

With right sides together, stitch one large ruffle short edge to the second large ruffle short edge. Repeat to connect the small ruffles.

Position each ruffle strip right side up on a flat work surface. Measure the small ruffle strip upper edge. This measurement should equal the recorded measurement. If the ruffle is longer, cut to the correct size. If the ruffle is shorter, add additional T-shirt fabric to equal the correct measurement.

With right sides together, stitch together the remaining large ruffle short edges to create a continuous strip. Repeat to stitch the small ruffle strip (3).

Serge- or zigzag-finish each ruffle upper edge.

Stitch a ½″ hem along each ruffle lower edge, using a narrow serger coverstitch or a double needle on a sewing machine. The lower 3½″ strip already has the manufacturer's hem, so finishing is unnecessary.

With right sides facing up, align the small ruffle upper edge ¼″ from the large ruffle upper edge; pin (4).

Stitch ³⁄₈″ from the large ruffle upper edge, using a long basting stitch and leaving a 4″-long tail at each end.

Fold the ruffle in half lengthwise and mark the center front, center back and each side seam. Fold the T-shirt in half lengthwise and mark the lower-edge center front, center back and side seams. Pin the ruffle wrong side to the T-shirt right side, aligning the marks.

Gently pull the thread tails to gather the ruffle edge, working from both ends toward the center until the ruffle fullness fits the T-shirt lower edge; pin.

Topstitch the ruffles to the T-shirt using a narrow zigzag stitch. Remove the gathering stitches; press.

Neck Ruffle

Supplies

- Long-sleeve T-shirt
- ¼ yard of sheer fabric, such as batiste, chiffon or voile
- 1¼"-wide strip of T-shirt knit fabric (length determined by neckline measurement)
- Thread: all-purpose & clear monofilament
- Removable fabric marker
- Serger

Prepare

Position the T-shirt front side up on a flat work surface and measure the neckline; record. Double the measurement to obtain the total length needed for the ruffle.

From the sheer fabric, cut a 3¾" x the fabric width strip. If needed, piece strips together to obtain the recorded measurement. With right sides together, stitch the strip short edges.

Set the serger to a narrow 3-thread overlock and thread with monofilament thread. Serge the ruffle strip lower edge. The monofilament thread will give the ruffle stiffness. Layer lightweight tear-away stabilizer under the fabric to help feed it through the serger smoothly.

Construct

Use ½" seam allowances unless otherwise noted. Allow the manufacturer's neckline to remain intact to prevent the neckline from stretching during construction.

With right sides together, stitch the remaining ruffle short edges, creating one continuous ruffle.

Baste ⅛" and then ¼" from the ruffle upper edge, leaving a 4"-long thread tail at each end.

Fold the ruffle in half lengthwise at the seam and mark the center front, center back and side seam. Fold the T-shirt in half lengthwise and mark the neckline center front and center back.

With right sides facing up, position the ruffle on the T-shirt neckline, matching the marks; pin. If the T-shirt has ribbing at the neckline, position the ruffle outside of the ribbing so it won't be included in the seam (5).

Gently pull the thread tails to gather the ruffle, working from both ends toward the center until the ruffle fullness fits the T-shirt neckline; pin, and then stitch.

Trim away the manufacturer's finished neckline, leaving a ¼" seam allowance.

Finish

To finish the neckline, cut the knit strip to match the neckline length, piecing the strip as needed to create the neckline binding.

With right sides together, position one binding long edge along the ruffle upper edge and T-shirt neckline; pin, and then stitch.

Fold the binding to the neckline wrong side; pin through only the knit layers.

Stitch the binding ⅜" from the neckline, moving the ruffle away from the stitching. Trim the binding close to the stitching.

Cut off the sleeve cuffs. Fold the raw edges to a ¾" sleeve length, and then stitch a ½" hem using a narrow coverstitch on a serger or a double needle on a sewing machine.

Tucks

Supplies

- Long-sleeve T-shirt (2 sizes larger or at least 5" additional fullness through bustline)
- 1¼"-wide strip of T-shirt knit fabric (length determined by neckline measurement)
- Matching all-purpose thread
- Removable fabric marker

Prepare

Fold the T-shirt in half lengthwise and mark the center front. Measure ¼", ¾", 1¼", 1¾" and 2¼" from the center line and draw a 6"-long line at each increment. Repeat to mark the opposite side (6).

Fold the T-shirt in half lengthwise and mark the center back. Measure ¼", ¾" and 1¼" from the center line and draw a 6"-long line at each increment. Repeat to mark the opposite side.

Construct

Use ½" seam allowances unless otherwise noted.

Fold the T-shirt in half lengthwise with wrong sides together, matching the first two tuck lines; pin. Stitch along the marked line, securing the stitches at each end. Repeat to stitch the remaining four tucks on the front and three tucks on the back. Press the tucks to the right side.

Baste along the T-shirt neckline. Trim away the manufacturer's finished neckline, leaving a ¼" seam allowance.

Finish

From the T-shirt fabric, cut the knit strip to match the neckline length, piecing the strip as needed to create the neckline binding. Bind the neckline as for the Neck Ruffle shirt.

If the T-shirt sleeves are too long, fold the sleeve hem to the wrong side to form a cuff or cut off the desired amount. Hem ½" using a narrow coverstitch on a serger or a double needle on a sewing machine.

If the T-shirt hem is too long, cut off the desired amount, and then hem the bottom using a narrow coverstitch or a double needle. ✄

T-SHIRT TIPS

- Use either a sewing machine or serger to stitch T-shirt knits.
- To prevent the stitches from breaking, use a medium stitch length and slightly stretch the fabric when feeding it through.
- When stitching knits on a serger, no additional stretch needs to be built into the stitches. If there are problems feeding the knit fabric through the machine, layer lightweight tear-away stabilizer between the fabric and feed dogs. It improves the fabric feed and helps produce even stitches.
- Use ballpoint needles, sizes 75/11 or 80/12, for either a sewing machine or serger.
- Save scraps of T-shirt knit for facings and bindings to make more T-shirts.

CUSTOM cardigan

{ by Cheryl Kuczek}

Upcycle an unflattering or secondhand sweater into a fun and trendy tie-front cardigan. Add wide coordinating trim and flared sleeves for a kimono-inspired look.

Supplies

- **Ready-made cotton, wool or mohair V-neck cardigan sweater**
- **1¹/₂ yards of coordinating woven print cotton fabric**
- **All-purpose thread**

Prepare

Select a V-neck cardigan sweater with a long, oversized fit and fine-gauge knit. A finer knit is easier to stitch to woven fabric trim. The sweater sleeves should be long and loose-fitting in order to create a flared kimono effect.

Construct

Use ¹/₄" seam allowances unless otherwise noted.

From the fabric, cut enough 2"-wide bias strips to create a continuous 70"-long strip. Piece together the strips along the short edges; press open the seams.

Pin-mark the new neckline and center-front edges on the sweater right side. The back neckline should be slightly lower than the original back neckline, and the front neckline should be deeper and wider than the original front neckline. Don't cut the sweater. The knit fabric needs to be stabilized by the woven fabric before cutting to prevent stretching and distortion.

Find the bias strip widthwise center. With right sides together, match the strip center to the new neckline center-back point. Position the strip along the new neckline and center-front edges according to the pin-marks; pin in place (1). Measure the distance from the trim to the sweater neckline edges, and then adjust the trim as needed until symmetrical.

Set the machine to a 2mm to 2.5mm stitch length. Stitch the strip to the sweater ¼″ from the strip upper edge.

Carefully cut the sweater even with the bias-strip upper edge. Fold the bias strip toward the sweater wrong side, enclosing the raw edges. Fold the remaining bias strip raw edge toward the wrong side, extending the strip folded edge approximately ⅛″ beyond the strip right-side edge; pin. Topstitch close to the strip right-side fold, catching the wrong-side fold in the stitching.

Turn the sweater to the wrong side. Try on the sweater to determine if any circumference adjustments are needed. Pin the front closed. If needed, pin the side seams to create a tapered shape. If altering the side seams, taper the sleeves the same amount to create a smooth transition from the sleeve to the side seam.

Stitch the new side and sleeve seams using a 2mm to 2.5mm stitch length. Set the machine to a three-step zigzag stitch, and then stitch ¼″ outside the first stitching line for additional security. Trim the seams ¼″ from the second stitching line.

Try on the sweater to determine the desired finished length; pin-mark. Measure the circumference at this point, and then add ½″; record.

From the fabric, cut one strip measuring 8″ x the recorded measurement. If the recorded measurement exceeds the fabric width, cut two strips measuring 8″ x the front lower-edge measurement plus ½″ and one strip measuring 8″ x the back lower-edge measurement plus ½″.

With right sides together, stitch the left-front strip to the back-strip left edge. Stitch the right-front strip to the back-strip right edge. Press open the seams.

Fold the lower-edge strip in half lengthwise, and then stitch the short edges. Trim the seam allowance and corners, and then turn the strip right side out; press.

Pin-mark the sweater 3¾″ from the desired finished lower edge. With right sides together, pin the lower-edge strip to the sweater, matching the center front edges and aligning the strip long open edge with the pin-marks. If applicable, match the strip side seams to the sweater side seams. Be careful not to stretch the sweater while pinning.

Stitch the strip open edge. Set the machine to a three-step zigzag stitch. Stitch the strip edge again using a ⅛″ seam allowance. Trim away the excess sweater fabric close to the second stitching line.

Fold the strip downward, and then lightly press along the trim right-side upper edge. Topstitch the trim upper edge using a standard straight stitch. Set the machine to a three-step zigzag or decorative stitch, and then stitch the strip perimeter, catching the seam allowance along the upper edge.

Try on the sweater, and then pin-mark the sleeves at the desired length. On the featured sample, the sleeves fall about 1½″ above the wristbone.

Measure the sleeve circumference at the desired length; record. Cut two fabric strips measuring 8″ x the recorded measurement plus ½″.

Fold one sleeve strip in half widthwise with right sides together. Stitch the 8″ open edge, forming a circle; press open the seam. With wrong sides together, fold the circle in half, aligning the raw edges; press (2). Repeat to stitch the remaining cuff.

Stitch one cuff to each sleeve in the same manner as the lower-edge strip, aligning the cuff seams with the sleeve seams. Trim away the excess sleeve fabric close to the stitching.

From the remaining fabric, cut one 2″ x 40″ strip. With right sides together, fold the strip in half lengthwise; press. Unfold, and then fold each long edge toward the wrong side foldline; press. Fold in half lengthwise again; press. Topstitch the long edges. Cut the strip into four 10″ ties.

Try on the sweater to determine the desired placement for each tie set along the center front edges; pin mark. Position one short end at each pin-mark on the sweater wrong side; stitch. Knot the remaining tie ends. ✄

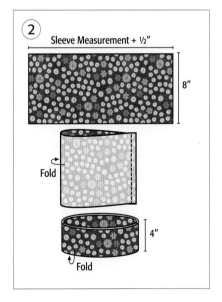

② Sleeve Measurement + ½″

8″

Fold

Fold

4″

Tip: Shop thrift stores for a sweater to alter. If you don't see one you like, check back in a week, as thrift stores constantly receive new donations.

HIP
Hardware

{ by Carol Zentgraf }

Add decorative and practical accents to garments
and accessories by adding grommets or eyelets.

Designer Details

Grommets and eyelets have been part of the garment industry since
the first metal versions replaced hand-sewn eyelets on corsets and
shoes in the early 1800s. Initially, grommets and eyelets were strictly
functional metal rings, but in recent years they've appeared in
designer garments in clever and innovative ways.

Grommets and eyelets are available in a variety of sizes and colors.
Use them on garments, accessories and home-décor projects to create
attractive and functional closures and openings, or creatively apply
them to projects as embellishments.

The terms "grommets" and "eyelets" are often used interchangeably,
as grommets and eyelets are very similar in appearance and serve many
of the same purposes. Both are available in a wide range of sizes and
finishes and feature a shaft that's inserted through a hole in fabric.
Grommets and eyelets are also sized in the same manner, with the
measurement on the package indicating the opening size.

Grommet & Eyelet Basics

Grommets consist of two parts: an upper ring with a decorative flange and shaft, and a washer that's placed on the fabric wrong side. They come in metal and plastic styles in sizes ranging from $3/8"$- to $1\ 9/16"$-diameter. Apply metal grommets to fabric using a setting tool and hammer or grommet pliers. When set into fabric, the shaft edge bends around the washer edge to secure. Use heavier metal grommets with several light- to mediumweight fabric layers or two heavyweight fabric layers reinforced with twill tape or interfacing. Plastic grommets feature an upper ring with a raised center on the underside that snaps into a ring with teeth on the wrong side. Use plastic grommets on light- to mediumweight fabrics.

Eyelets range in size from $5/32"$- to $7/16"$-diameter. Set eyelets using pliers or an eyelet-setting tool. Smaller eyelets are available in novelty shapes, such as stars, hearts and flowers, as well as the traditional round shape, and in a wide range of colors. They consist of one piece and have a shaft with a scored edge that splits to grip the fabric when set. Larger eyelets consist of two pieces and feature a shank that's secured with a pronged washer on the fabric wrong side. Small eyelets are best suited for lightweight fabric or even paper. Use larger eyelets with several light- to mediumweight fabric layers or two heavyweight fabric layers, reinforced with twill tape or interfacing.

When beginning a project, determine if the end-use for the grommets or eyelets will be functional or purely decorative. Before setting the grommets or eyelets, audition them on the fabric to determine the spacing and design placement.

TRICKS OF THE TRADE

Keep these tips in mind for best results when planning a design and selecting fabric appropriate for grommets and eyelets.

• Select fabric that has a fairly tight weave or is tightly knit. Loose weaves don't provide enough support for the weight of the metal, and many knits stretch and allow the grommet or eyelet to pop out. Avoid placing grommets or eyelets in any garment areas that will stretch.

• When using grommets or eyelets on knit fabrics, make the smallest hole possible, and then stretch the fabric tightly around the shank.

• Select grommets or eyelets that are the appropriate size for the fabric weight and follow the manufacturer's recommendations for the number of fabric layers to use.

• Use interfacing to reinforce the fabric area where eyelets or grommets are applied whenever possible. To stabilize areas that are difficult to interface, adhere a small fusible interfacing circle to the fabric wrong side at the grommet or eyelet placement point. Or cut a small piece of tear-away stabilizer and place it around the shank on the fabric wrong side before adding the washer; trim any excess stabilizer. For extra reinforcement along an edge, stitch twill tape along the grommet placement marking before setting the grommets or eyelets.

• Apply grommets or eyelets before or after constructing the project. If adding them before construction, avoid placing them too close to seams or areas that will be topstitched. If adding them after construction, use grommets or eyelets designed to be set with an applicator tool rather than pliers if they will be placed more than 1" from an edge.

Setting Specifics

For snap-together grommets and eyelets, use small, sharp scissors to cut the hole in the fabric and prepare it for setting. For other grommet or eyelet styles, refer to the package for the specific corresponding setting tool or pliers needed. Many kits include a setting tool or refills, as well as a template or washer for marking the hole. Or mark the hole by using a fine-tip fabric marker to trace the grommet inner edge.

Before setting grommets or eyelets on your project, practice setting them on fabric scraps. Experiment to determine how hard you need to strike the setting tool with the hammer or how hard you need to squeeze the pliers. Too much force distorts the metal, while not enough force results in an insufficient attachment.

To set a snap-together grommet, mark the grommet center position on the fabric right side. Position the template over the mark; trace, and then cut out the hole. Insert the grommet raised center in the hole from the fabric right side. Snap the grommet prong side in place on the fabric wrong side.

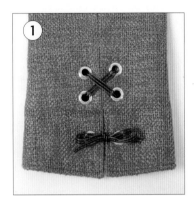

Tip: Use grommets to reinforce a drawstring opening on a garment or handbag. Or use them to create durable holes on a belt.

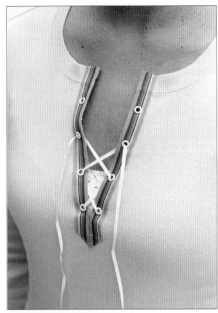

To set a grommet or eyelet using tools included in the package, trace the template or mark the position by tracing the grommet or eyelet inner edge. Cut out the hole, and then insert the shaft through the hole from the fabric right side. If there's a ring or washer, slide it onto the shaft, sandwiching the fabric. Place the setting-tool anvil on a hard protected surface. Position the eyelet or grommet on the anvil; insert the tool in the center. For small eyelets, hammer gently to split the eyelet center, attaching it to the fabric, washer or ring. For large eyelets and grommets, hammer forcefully, rotating the anvil one-quarter turn between strikes, allowing the shank to evenly roll over the washer edge to secure.

To set a grommet or eyelet using pliers, mark the grommet center position on the fabric. Follow the manufacturer's instructions, using the pliers to punch a hole in the fabric, and then set the grommet or eyelet.

Creative Closure

Use grommets or eyelets with lacing to replace a buttoned or zipped closure on any jacket or vest pattern where the front edges abut rather than overlap. Or use grommets and ribbon to create a decorative laced edge on garment with an open front.

Construct the jacket or vest following the pattern guidesheet, applying interfacing to the front-opening edges.

Align the garment front edges on a flat work surface. Mark evenly-spaced, parallel placements along each edge, positioning the grommet edges at least $1/2''$ from the fabric finished edge.

Apply the grommets or eyelets at the placement marks.

Lace ribbon through the grommet openings as desired, tying the ends together at the upper edge. Or lace ribbon through the openings along each edge individually, tacking the ends at the upper and lower edges.

Laced Seam

Highlight a sleeve seam, side seam or vent using grommets or eyelets.

To add grommets or eyelets for lacing along a seam, finish the seam opening edge with an interfaced facing for added stability.

Mark the grommet placements along the seam as desired, and then apply the grommets. Lace ribbon through the grommet openings (1).

New Neckline

Dress up a basic T-shirt by quickly creating a laced neckline opening.

At the center-front neckline edge, mark a vertical line the desired opening length.

Cut along the line. Serge- or zigzag-finish the cut edges.

Position a ribbon along the neckline opening, beginning and ending at the neckline upper edge and creating a mi-

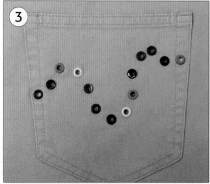

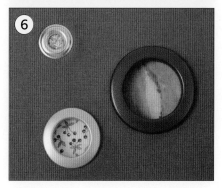

tered corner at the opening lower edge; pin. Trim and fold the ribbon ends ½″ toward the shirt wrong side; pin.

Mark the eyelet placements along the ribbon; apply the eyelets. Thread a ribbon or cord through the openings.

Embellishment Options

Use grommets and eyelets in a variety of ways to embellish a finished garment.

Accent the edges of a front opening, hem, neckline, pocket or sleeve by applying evenly-spaced grommets or eyelets along the finished interfaced edge (2). Leave them open or thread ribbon, fabric strips or trim through the openings; tack the ribbon ends or tie them into a bow.

Apply a variety of grommets and eyelets to any garment area to create a free-form design (3). Or accent fabric or embroidery motifs with grommets or eyelets (4).

Cut out felt or suede appliqués, and then attach the center using a grommet or extra-large eyelet (5).

Create the illusion of a filled grommet or eyelet by positioning matching or contrasting fabric behind the opening (6). Either glue the fabric backing in place using fabric adhesive, or stitch the fabric in place around the grommet or eyelet perimeter. ✄

SOURCES

The Junk Jeans People provided grommets: junkjeanspeople.com.

Prym Consumer USA provided grommets, eyelets and tools: dritz.com.

OFF THE CUFF

{ by Carol Zentgraf}

Add zing to basic capri pants with quick and cute cuff treatments. Use just one pattern to create five fun takes on a summer wardrobe staple.

Reverse Facing

Use bright print fabric and ribbon to add a clever cuff facing.

Supplies

- Capri pant pattern (such as Simplicity 5259, view B)
- Fabric & notions (as indicated on pattern envelope)
- $1/8$ yard of coordinating print fabric (See "Sources.")
- Pattern tracing cloth
- $1^1/2$ yards of $1/4$"-wide ribbon

Cut & Construct

Cut out the pattern pieces, following the pattern guidesheet.

Follow the pattern guidesheet to construct the capris, but leave the leg side seams unstitched.

Trim $3/8$" from each leg lower edge.

Create the Facing

On the pant front leg pattern, draw a line $2^5/8$" from and parallel to the lower edge.

Trace the lower edge and drawn line on a piece of tracing cloth. Trace the side seams up to the drawn line. This is the front facing pattern. Repeat to trace the back pant leg lower edge and create the back facing pattern.

Cut out the patterns, and then cut two front and two back facings each from the print fabric.

Align one front and one back facing with right sides together. Stitch the inner leg seam; press open. Repeat to stitch the remaining front and back facings.

With the wrong sides facing up, align the inner leg seams and lower edges (1).

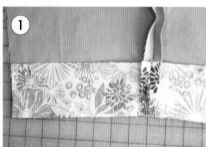

Using a $5/8$" seam allowance, stitch the facing lower and side edges through both layers; clip and trim the corners (2).

Repeat to stitch the remaining facing to the remaining pant leg.

With right sides together, stitch the pant side seams from the waistline to the facing upper edges.

Turn the pants right side out, and then fold the facings toward the right side; press.

Finish

Cut two ribbon lengths equal to the cuff circumference plus 1". Position one ribbon along one facing raw upper edge, overlapping the ends over the inner leg seam; pin. Stitch the ribbon long edges through all layers (3). Repeat to stitch ribbon over the remaining facing upper edge.

DISTRESSED FOR LESS

Do you or your children love the destroyed-jeans look? Create the look yourself at a fraction of retail prices.

• Purchase inexpensive plain jeans that fit loosely as most jeans shrink progressively with each laundering. Avoid Lycra blends if you want the faded look since Lycra is destroyed by chlorine bleach.

• Use scissors or a knife to cut holes or rips as desired. One"- to 4" square, oval, or round shapes work well. Natural wear areas that develop into holes might include the knees, thigh region and lower back pockets.

• Use a rasp, sandpaper or large nail file to distress the hole edges, hems, pockets and fly.

• Wash the jeans in hot water with detergent on a long heavy-duty agitation cycle. Add old towels or another pair of jeans to the wash for extra abrasion. For a faded look, add chlorine bleach or Rit Dye Fast Fade. Add some denim patches to the same wash to fray the edges. Repeat the washing and bleaching process until you like the look. Then add a large handful of salt to the last wash cycle to help set the color.

• Apply patches, with or without fusible web, to the right or wrong side of the jeans. Use scraps from old jeans, new denim fabric or contrast fabric for the patches. Leave the edges frayed.

• For extra durability, darn over the patches with matching or contrasting thread. Try Jeans Stitch variegated thread or traditional white, orange or gold jeans thread. Avoid stitching over the frayed areas.

• Hand patch and/or darn the holes in hard-to-reach areas, such as pockets. For an extra handcrafted look, use contrasting thread and slightly large, uneven stitches.

• When the jeans are complete, wash in cold water on the gentle cycle and air dry to preserve the destroyed look and avoid further shrinkage.

Darning eggs

approximately ¹/₂″ beyond the patch edges. Rotate the garment 90°, and then stitch another set of parallel rows at right angles to the first **(5)**. Don't worry about being precise. Use the reverse control instead of pivoting at the end of each row.

Use traditional hand-darning methods for small holes in knits and fine fabrics.

Spread the hole area over something small and firm, such as the bottom of a tumbler, a smooth stone or a hard-boiled egg. Our ancestors used darning eggs, some with handles, which look like wooden baby rattles (see above).

Using matching thread, stitch a small running stitch around the hole perimeter.

Starting approximately ¹/₂″ outside of the hole perimeter, stitch toward the center of the hole with a small running stitch. When you reach the hole,

move the thread across to the other side and stitch to ¹/₂″ outside the hole perimeter. Turn the work 180° and stitch parallel to the first row, skipping across the hole and stitching ¹/₂″ further to form a border. Continue stitching closely spaced parallel rows until the hole is covered.

Rotate the patch 90°. Stitch in the border, but instead of skipping across the hole area, weave the needle under and over the first set of threads, continuing with ¹/₂″ of running stitches on the other side of the hole. Pivot and continue to stitch. Weave and stitch until the hole area and border are completely filled. The closely spaced rows and weaving process form a woven fabric that will cover the hole **(6)**. ✂

SOURCES
Barbara Deckert writes more about fixing sewing mistakes in *Sewing 911: Practical and Creative Rescues for Sewing Emergencies,* from The Taunton Press.

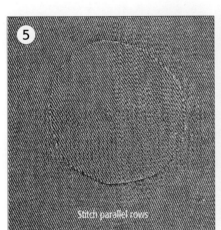
⑤ Stitch parallel rows

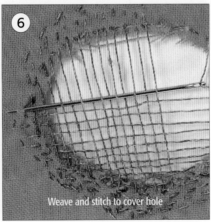
⑥ Weave and stitch to cover hole

GOT PATCHES? SHOW 'EM OFF!

Showcase your collection of decorative patches, such as the punk rock band patches shown here.

Select a favorite jacket from your wardrobe or purchase a new or used jacket. The patches can cover any rips or moth holes. Leave the patch raw edges unfinished for a deconstructed look.

To fuse the patches, apply fusible web to the wrong sides. Arrange the patches on the jacket and fuse in place.

Without using fusible web, or for extra durability and a decorative effect, pin the patches to the jacket as desired. Then use a contrasting or embroidery thread and blindstitch the patches to the jacket. Make the stitches uneven to accentuate the hand-sewn look.

Tip: If a garment is lined, hand stitch patches only through the outside fabric layer and avoid catching the lining.

CUTE AS A
BUTTON

{ by Dawn Anderson Schons }

Hand embroidered
buttons are a great
fashion accessory.
Customize the button
designs to accent a
special garment or
craft project.

Supplies

- 8″ squares of mediumweight nonstretch fabric
- Lightweight fusible interfacing
- 4″-diameter hand embroidery hoop
- 1¹/₂″-, 1¹/₈″- and ³/₄″-diameter covered button kits
- Double-stick tape
- All-purpose thread
- Embroidery floss
- Temporary spray adhesive
- Needles: beading, hand embroidery, hand sewing (size 8) and tapestry (size 26)
- Removable fabric marker
- Pounce wheel
- Beads and sequins (optional)
- Removable ink transfer paper (optional)

Getting Started

Select an embroidery design from page 46. Cut the embroidery floss to 12″ to 14″ lengths. Separate the floss lengths into fewer strands as instructed for the selected button design. For blended thread colors, separate the six strands and retwist with the additional colors.

Press the fabric square. Select the desired circle template from page 46. Trace the circle on the fabric wrong side. Baste along the traced line (1). Transfer the embroidery design to the fabric right side inside the basting stitching.

From the lightweight interfacing, cut one circle. Center the interfacing circle within the traced circle on the fabric wrong side; fuse. Hoop the fabric (2).

Embroidery

Begin embroidering using a small backstitch and end by tunneling under a few stitches on the embroidery wrong side to secure the thread.

When the embroidery is complete, remove the fabric from the hoop. Center the circle template over the embroidery design, aligning the center dot with the design center; pin. Cut out the fabric circle.

Position a small piece of double stick tape over the blank button shell. Center the embroidered design over the button shell and carefully finger-press the fabric to adhere it to the shell.

Position small pieces of double stick tape along the button shell inner edges. Fold the fabric toward the button shell inside; finger-press.

Tip: Press cotton embroidery floss using steam to remove wrinkles.

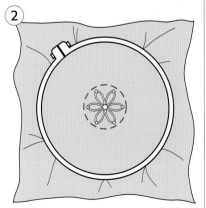

Small Rose

Large Rose

Starfish

Autumn Leaf

Small Daisy

Large Daisy

Wagon Wheel

Spiral

Victorian Fan

Snowflake

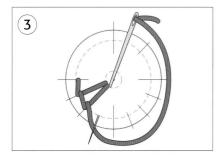

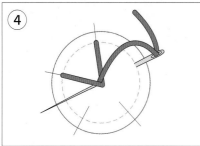

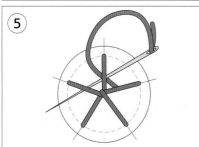

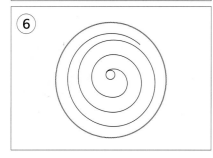

Remove the basting thread. Attach the button backs, following the manufacturer's instructions.

Attach the beads or sequins using a backstitch. Tie a knot under the bead to hide the thread tails.

Wagon Wheel
Supplies

• 8" square of dark brown linen

• 6 strands of tan embroidery floss

• 1¹/₈" fabric-covered button blank

• Brown bead

Baste ¹/₈" inside the outer basted circle. Mark the circle center. Baste a small circle ¹/₈" outside the center mark. Divide the circle into quarters using pins, thread marks or removable ink transfer paper.

Blanket stitch around the circle using the inner two circles as stitch length guides (3). Remove the basting thread. Cover the button; hand stitch a bead at the circle center.

Starfish
Supplies

• 8" square of light blue linen

• 6 strands of tan embroidery floss

• 6 strands of blended embroidery floss: 4 peach, 2 dark tan

• 1¹/₈" fabric-covered button blank

Divide the circle into fifths and mark the center. Baste ¹/₁₆" inside the outer circle. Using the tan floss, straight stitch the star spokes. Bring the thread up from the fabric wrong side at the circle center, catching the first stitch in the center. Straight stitch the remaining spokes (4).

With the blended thread, finish with the spider web stitch. Bring the threaded needle up through the center from the fabric wrong side. Stitch over the first straight stitch and guide the needle over and under the subsequent threads (5), alternating to achieve a web look. Leave the spoke ends visible.

Spiral
Supplies

• 8" square of lavender cotton

• 9" length of multi-colored eyelash yarn

• 3 strands of purple embroidery floss

• 1¹/₂" fabric-covered button blank

• Temporary spray adhesive

Using a removable fabric marker, trace the spiral line template (6) onto the fabric right side.

Fold one eyelash yarn end 1/4". Using temporary spray adhesive, align the yarn with the circle center. Follow the spiral and couch the eyelash yarn in place using the purple embroidery floss.

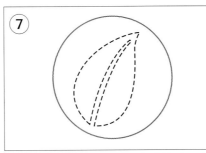

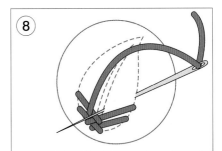

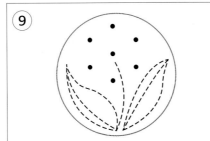

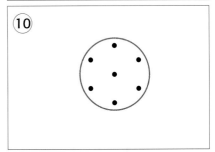

Autumn Leaf

Supplies

• 8" square of burgundy cotton

• 4 strands of blended floss: 3 orange, 1 dark orange

• 3 strands of yellow embroidery floss

• 1¹/₂" fabric-covered button blank

Trace the leaf template to the fabric right side (7). Using the blended thread, begin the leaf stitch at the design lower edge.

Repeat the stitch sequence toward the leaf upper edge, evenly spacing the stitches (8).

Using the yellow floss, stitch small French knots around the leaf.

Daisies

Supplies

• 8" square of green linen

• 3 strands each of embroidery floss: white, dark green, and orange

• 1¹/₂" fabric-covered button blank (for large flower and leaves button)

• ³/₄" fabric-covered button blank (for small flower button)

Trace the leaf template, center line markings and the stem onto the fabric right side. Trace seven dots for the flower center and the petal tips (9). Trace seven dots on the small button fabric circle (10).

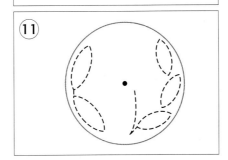

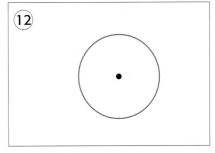

For the large button, stitch the leaf design as for the Autumn Leaf.

Create the flowers using the lazy daisy stitch. Stitch three French knots over the large button flower center, and one French knot over the small button flower center. Connect the flower to the leaves using a stem stitch.

Roses

Supplies

• 8" square cream linen

• 3 strands each of embroidery floss: dark green, red

• 1¹/₂" fabric-covered button blank (for large flower and leaves button)

• ³/₄" fabric-covered button blank (for small flower button)

For the large button, trace the leaves, the stem and the flower center onto the fabric right side (11). For the small button, transfer the center dot (12). For the large or small roses, use the bullion stitch with a small backstitch.

Guide the needle out slightly where it first entered the fabric. Twist the working thread around the needle point, until the twist length matches the backstitch length. The wrapped threads should be snug, but loose enough that the needle eye will pass though easily.

Holding the coiled thread, turn the needle back to where it was inserted and insert again.

Pull the thread through until the stitches lay flat on the fabric surface.

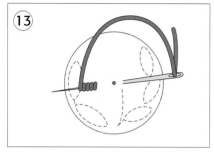

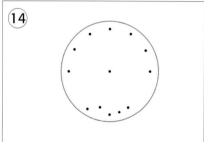

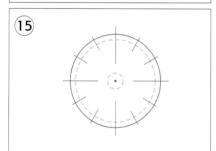

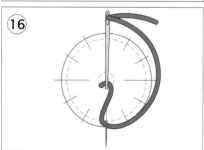

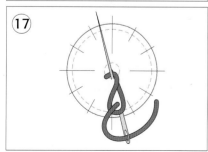

Make the first set of bullion stitches small, with five wraps around the needle (13). Increase the number of wraps and the backstitch size to stitch the larger petals. Repeat the bullion stitch around the rose center.

Stitch a French knot at the flower center. For the large rose button, fill in the leaf outlines using the leaf stitch. Connect the leaves and embroider the stem with the stem stitch.

Victorian Fan
Supplies

• 8″ square of pink satin

• 3 strands each of embroidery floss: gold metallic, light blue

• 1¹⁄₈″ fabric-covered button blank

• Gold sequin

• Gold bead

Trace the center and fan points onto the fabric right side (14). Using the blue thread, blanket stitch from the center out to the fan points. Straight stitch in a long and short pattern below the button center. With the gold thread, zigzag the fan top. Stitch medium-sized French knots below the straight stitches, and stitch small French knots in between the fan sections. Stitch the sequin and bead after attaching the button back.

Snowflake
Supplies

• 8″ square of navy satin

• 3 strands of silver-gray embroidery floss

• 1¹⁄₈″ fabric-covered button blank

• Silver sequin

• Silver seed bead

Baste a circle ¹⁄₈″ inside the outer circle. Mark the circle center. Baste a circle ¹⁄₈″ outside the center, creating a ¹⁄₄″-diameter circle at the center. Divide circle into quarters using pins, thread marks or removable ink transfer paper. Divide each quarter circle into three parts, creating 12 circle divisions (15).

Basque stitch by bringing the thread up from the fabric wrong side along the basted circle. Move the needle over slightly to the right and take a stitch from the inner circle to the outer circle.

Wrap the thread around the needle in a figure eight motion (16). Hold the thread down with your thumb and pull gently. Take the next stitch along the outer circle to secure the loop (similar to the lazy daisy).

Bring up the needle next to the upper thread loop. Pull the thread through (17).

Continue working the Basque stitch, using the 12 divisions as a stitch placement guide. Stitch the bead and sequin at the button center after the button parts are joined. ✄

A STITCH IN TIME { by Sharon Boggon }

Learn basic embroidery stitches to help create beautiful embellished buttons.

Blanket Stitch: The blanket stitch is worked from left to right over two imaginary lines. Bring the thread to the fabric right side along the lower line. Insert the needle on the upper line **(A)**, making a straight downward motion. Loop the thread under the needle point. Pull the needle through. Repeat **(B)**.

Couching Stitch: Position the surface thread on the fabric, as desired. Bring the thread up from the fabric wrong side with a large-eyed needle. Take small, straight stitches over the thick thread and back through the fabric **(C)**. Secure both ends with a few small stitches. Don't clip the heavy thread too close, otherwise it will appear on the embroidery surface.

French Knot: Bring the needle up from the fabric wrong side and hold the thread taut with your thumb. Twist the needle around the thread twice **(D)**. Holding the thread firmly, insert the needle into the fabric a small distance from where the thread emerged **(E)**. Push the knot down the needle shaft firm against the fabric **(F)**. Pull the thread through to the fabric wrong side (G).

Lazy Daisy Stitch: Bring the needle up from the fabric wrong side **(H)** and hold the thread with your thumb. Insert the needle back into where it first came out, and

then guide the needle back through the fabric a small distance from the center **(I)**. With the thread wrapped under the needle point, pull the needle through the fabric; fasten the loop with a small stitch **(J)**. To make a flower, stitch in a circle with each stitch radiating outward to form petals **(K)**.

Leaf Stitch: Bring the needle up from the fabric wrong side **(L)** and hold the thread down with your thumb. Insert the needle a little to the right on the same level and make a small stitch in a downward diagonal motion so that the needle point appears on the center line. Keeping the thread under the needle point, pull the thread through the fabric. Make a second stitch in the same manner **(M)**. Insert the needle a little to the left and make a small diagonal stitch so that the needle point comes out on the center line. Keep the thread under the needle point; pull the thread through the fabric to make the stitch **(N)**. Repeat the stitch, alternating from side to side **(O)**.

Stem Stitch: Working from left to right, bring the thread out on the line, as desired. Straight stitch through the fabric and angle the needle backward to bring it up to the first stitch lower edge. Pull the thread through the fabric. Straight stitch again, bringing the needle out a little to the second stitch lower edge. Repeat this back and forth movement along the line **(P)**.

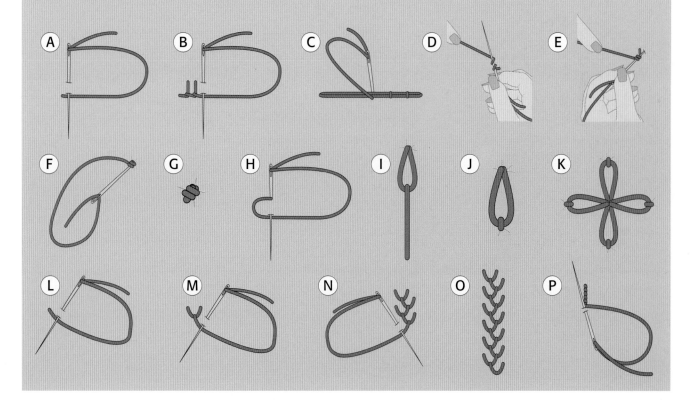

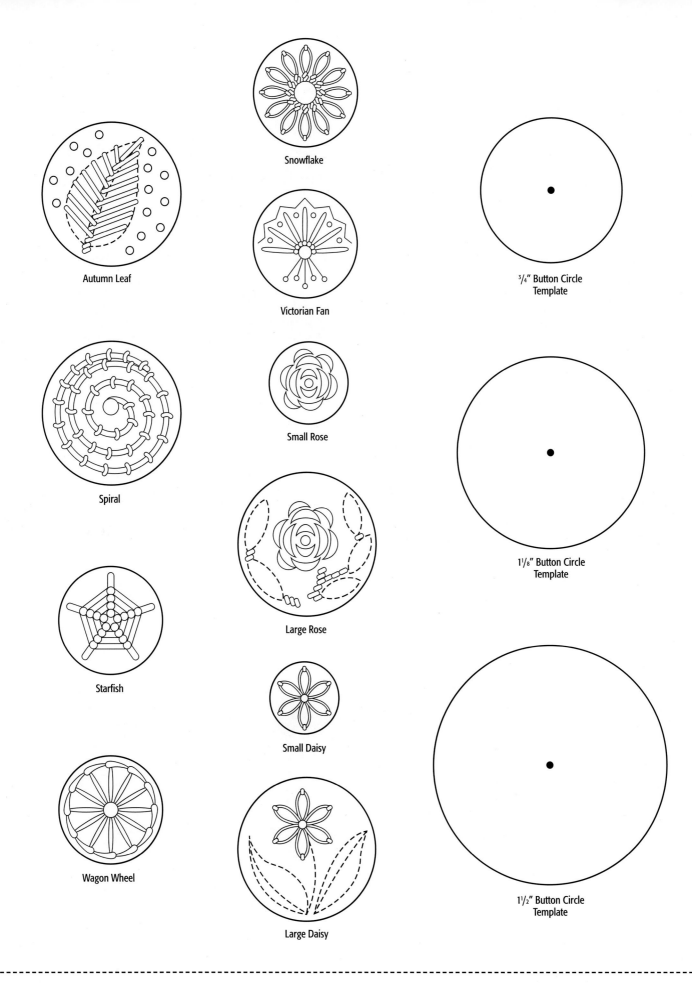

Autumn Leaf

Snowflake

Victorian Fan

3/4" Button Circle
Template

Spiral

Small Rose

Large Rose

1 1/8" Button Circle
Template

Starfish

Small Daisy

Wagon Wheel

Large Daisy

1 1/2" Button Circle
Template

DISCHARGE { by Dana Bontrager } EMBELLISHMENT

Discharging, or removing the color from fabric or paper, is a technique that creates images or abstract designs by removing the fabric surface dye. Read on to discover this interesting and unique technique.

Discharge Innovation

Before the invention of discharge paste, discharge embellishment was done using chlorine bleach. Bleach only works on certain fabrics, destroys some fibers and is difficult to control, forcing the user to work quickly. Thanks to discharge paste, discharge embellishment is simple and fun. It removes only the dye particles from reactive, direct and acid dyes, while leaving the fabric fibers completely unharmed. Discharge paste also enables easy stamping, stenciling or painting directly onto fabric without the use of thickening agents. A wide variety of fabrics are compatible with the discharging technique. Test discharging on scrap fabric first to ensure desired results.

Techniques

STAMPING

Use stamps with simple, large designs, as small details will not show clearly (1). Apply the discharge paste to the stamp with a sponge or foam brayer, and stamp by pressing firmly down on the fabric. Use a towel or a thin felt scrap under the fabric to protect the surface underneath. Depending on how evenly the discharge paste is applied to the stamp, the design may appear thicker or thinner in some areas. To avoid this, use less paste and avoid heavy globs when applying.

STENCILING

Position the stencil over the fabric. Apply the discharge paste to the fabric with a foam sponge, employing a tapping motion over the stencil. Use a small amount of discharge paste and add more as needed. Heavier applications will saturate the design, resulting in less detail.

PAINTING

Paint the discharge paste directly onto the fabric, using a soft foam brush for swirls and swoops, or a stiff brush for an abstract effect.

DOODLING

Fill a small applicator bottle with the discharge paste to doodle on fabric. Write names, make curlicues and dots or draw pictures. Keep the bottle tip close to the fabric surface for best results. Avoid shaking the bottle, as this will cause air bubbles that splatter and break up smooth lines. To keep the paste near the tip, tap it gently to force the paste downward and the air toward the top (2).

SPLATTERING

Apply discharge paste on a toothbrush or fingernail brush. Run a finger across the brush toward your body to splatter the paste across the fabric. If you run your finger across the brush away from you, it will splatter on you. Thin the discharge paste with water, if necessary. Do not apply the discharge paste by spraying it from a spray bottle.

LEAF IMPRESSIONS

Use real leaves just like stamps to create a beautiful effect (3). Choose leaves that are flat and have prominent veining. Avoid leaves that are prickly or extremely fragile. Using a foam brush, apply the discharge paste to the leaf back side, where the veins are most prominent. Carefully place the leaf paste side down on the fabric. Cover the leaf with a piece of scrap paper and rub from the center out. Remove the paper and carefully lift the leaf from the fabric.

PRINTED FABRICS

Discharge on printed fabrics with small designs; busy or large printed designs will not show the discharging detail. A small, dense cotton print may have an interesting effect. Often a screen printed design will only discharge slightly (screen print inks sit on the surface and are usually applied heavily for saturation), but the background will discharge more, creating a shadow effect.

Finishing

The discharge paste may dry in a few minutes or overnight, depending on the thickness of application. Once completely dry, iron the design with a steam iron on the correct fabric setting. The steam removes the color, so set the iron to high steam. Wash or rinse the fabric to remove any excess paste.

Color Surprise

Fabrics react differently to discharging; most fabrics will lighten, but sometimes the color will change completely. A light green fabric may turn blue, denim blue may become fuchsia and a lime green could turn purple. Test on scrap fabric similar to the chosen fabric to ensure desired results.

Discharging on Paper

The discharge technique works on colored papers. Use the same techniques to apply the discharge paste for stamping, stenciling and splattering. Keep the application as light as possible, as soaked paper will soften and become fragile. When the design is dry, press it with heat from an iron to remove the color. Do not use steam on paper. ✄

SOURCES
Dana Marie Design Co. #1025 Sahara
Dana Marie Design Co. #1002 To Dye for duster

BOBBINWORK
IN BLOOM

{ by Sara Boughner }

Combine free-motion appliqué and bobbinwork with
modern floral fabrics to create a stylish weekend travel tote.

TIP: When stitching with invisible thread, always test-stitch on a fabric scrap. If the stitch isn't forming correctly, slightly loosen the upper tension and test-stitch again.

Easy Embellishment

While standard sewing, the machine feed dogs move the fabric from front to back under the presser foot as the needle moves up and down, creating stitches in a straight line. While free-motion stitching, the feed dogs are lowered so you can move the fabric in any direction. This makes it easy to stitch around free-form appliqué shapes, circles and other motifs.

While there's a vast variety of decorative thread and yarns to use for embellishment, you're usually limited to using a fiber that's narrow enough to fit through the needle eye. Bobbinwork opens up the possibilities for wider and bulkier thread, yarn and ribbon because the fabric is stitched from the wrong side, allowing the embellishment fiber to appear on the fabric right side.

Free-motion appliqué and bobbinwork techniques work well together to create a unique embellished effect. Eliminate the difficulty of stitching the bobbinwork from the fabric wrong side by using the appliqué stitching lines as a handy stitching guide.

Supplies
- Oversized tote bag pattern (See "Sources.")
- Solid fabric for exterior body (amount according to pattern envelope)
- Large-scale floral print lining fabric (amount according to pattern envelope, plus ¼ yard; see "Sources")
- ¼ yard of coordinating large-scale floral print fabric (See "Sources.")
- Interfacing & notions (according to pattern envelope)
- Fusible web (See "Sources.")
- Thread: all-purpose, heavyweight decorative & invisible
- Free-motion foot
- Accessory bobbin case (See "Sources.")
- Extra empty bobbins
- Tapestry needle
- Piping trimming tool (optional; see "Sources")

Prepare

Cut out the pattern pieces from the fabric, lining and interfacing, following the pattern guidesheet.

Fuse the interfacing pieces to the corresponding fabric pieces, following the manufacturer's instructions.

Construct the piping following the pattern guidesheet. Use a piping trimming tool to easily trim the piping seam allowance, if desired.

Stitch the tote front- and back-panel pleats, following the pattern guidesheet.

Embellish

From the floral print fabrics, select several flower motifs of varying sizes to fussy-cut for the appliqués. The featured bag has five large and five small flower appliqués on each panel.

Adhere the fusible web to the floral fabric wrong side, following the manufacturer's instructions. Fussy-cut the selected motifs from the fused fabric.

BEAUTIFUL BOBBINWORK

Follow these tips for bobbinwork success:

- To prevent thread breakage, avoid using very thin or delicate thread in the needle. During bobbinwork, the upper thread has to work slightly harder to pull the bobbin thread out of the bobbin and onto the fabric.

- Test-stitch on an interfaced fabric scrap to determine the correct tension settings for bobbinwork. If the stitch isn't forming correctly, try slightly loosening the upper tension.

- When adjusting bobbin tension, always use an accessory bobbin case. The original bobbin case tension is set by the manufacturer to accommodate a range of standard bobbin threads. These settings should only be adjusted by a trained service technician with the proper tool, so invest in a second bobbin case for experimenting.

- For a bolder effect, use coordinating lightweight yarn or silk ribbon up to 6mm-wide to create the bobbinwork.

- Always use the machine to fill the bobbin rather than doing it by hand. If your embellishment fiber is too thick to fit on the horizontal spool pin, use an upright spool pin. If you don't have an upright spool pin, or the embellishment fiber is not on a spool, place it on a flat surface and thread it through the normal path used to wind the bobbin. Carefully guide the fiber as the bobbin winds. If it's too thick to pass through the bobbin tension discs, apply gentle pressure by guiding it between your thumb and forefinger as the bobbin winds.

- Experiment with decorative stitches when doing bobbinwork. Avoid dense or heavy stitches, such as a satin stitch, triple stitch or any pattern in which the stitches overlap.

- Make sure the fabric is adequately stabilized for bobbinwork. Select the stabilizer appropriate for the chosen fabric weight. (The featured bag panels are interfaced, so additional stabilizer isn't necessary.)

- Stitch in open patterns and shapes, as bulky bobbin thread doesn't allow for fine details and perfect angles.

Audition the appliqués on the bag front and back panel right sides until satisfied with the placement; pin. Leave at least 2″ free around the appliqué edges to allow for the bag seam allowance.

Remove the fusible-web paper backing from the appliqués; fuse.

Thread the machine with invisible thread in the needle and matching all-purpose thread in the bobbin. Install a free-motion foot and refer to the manual to set the machine for free-motion stitching.

With the right side facing up, free-motion stitch each appliqué as desired. Stitch the perimeter, around the petals or stitch only at the flower center to secure each appliqué.

Fill several bobbins with heavyweight decorative thread. Load one bobbin into an accessory bobbin case. Test to make sure that the thread easily pulls through the bobbin. If it's difficult to pull, loosen the bobbin tension by turning the bobbin case screw to the left. Install the bobbin case.

Thread the needle with all-purpose thread in a color similar to the bobbin thread.

Place an interfaced fabric scrap right side down on the machine. Test-stitch the fabric scrap, and then tighten the upper tension if necessary.

TIP: Create eye-catching effects by using metallic or variegated heavyweight thread for the bobbinwork.

With the fabric wrong side facing up, place one bag panel on the machine. If desired, re-engage the feed dogs and set the machine for standard stitching, or keep the settings for free-motion stitching. Manually turn the hand wheel toward you to bring up the bobbin thread through the fabric. Leave a long thread tail to prevent the thread from jamming under the throatplate while stitching.

Stitch each appliqué, using the original appliqué stitching lines as a placement guide. Follow the appliqué stitching lines, or stitch new lines as desired.

Move from one appliqué to another continuously, or individually stitch each appliqué. Leave long thread tails at the stitching beginning and ending.

Finish

When the bobbinwork is complete, remove the fabric from the machine and use a tapestry needle to pull the thread tails to the fabric wrong side. Knot the thread tails, and then trim the excess.

Finish constructing the bag, following the pattern guidesheet. ✂

SOURCES

Amy Butler Design provided the Field Bag & Tote pattern: amybutlerdesign.com.

BonnieMcCaffery.com provided the YLI Candlelight Yarn: (570) 775-7118, bonniemccaffery.com.

Pfaff provided the creative Bobbin Case: (800) 446-2333, pfaffusa.com.

Pieces Be With You carries the Groovin' Piping Trimming Tool Grande: piecesbewithyou.com.

Superior Threads carries Halo metalized textured polyester thread: (800) 499-1777; superiorthreads.com.

Westminster Fibers provided the Amy Butler Soul Blossoms and solid fabric: (866) 907-3305, westminsterfibers.com.

YLI carries invisible monofilament thread: (803) 985-3100; ylicorp.com.

FELTED Finery

{ by Susan Beck }

Needle felting or punching is a fun and simple free-motion embellishment technique. Use needle felting to add color, develop unique textures, make fabric collages or create backgrounds for quilting and embroidery. Read on to create a cozy neck warmer decorated with a colorful needle-felted design.

Needle-Felting Techniques

To needle felt by hand, place a piece of foam or a specially designed mat behind the base fabric to punch into and protect the work surface. Use a single felting needle to punch the fiber into the base fabric, or use a tool containing multiple needles to speed up the process (1). To create outlines or small details, use one needle or a tool with two needles.

To use a needle-felting machine or attachment, arrange the fibers as desired on the base fabric. Anchor the fibers using a hand–felting needle if needed. Drop the machine feed dogs, and then move the fabric as the needles punch

the fibers (2). The machine doesn't require any thread to secure the fibers. In fact, the bobbin and thread hook are completely removed. Most felting machines or attachments have three to 12 needles. The machine motor and multiple needles makes needle felting very quick, but use a slower speed and/ or fewer needles when felting detailed or delicate designs.

Supplies

- 1 to 1½ yards of 100% wool fabric
- Multicolored wool roving or yarn
- Needle-felting machine or hand felting supplies

- Matching all-purpose thread
- Large decorative button
- Chalk marker
- Fusible interfacing
- Narrow cord for buttonhole

Felted Neck Warmer

Wear this felted wool neck warmer over your coat collar to keep the wind out and the warmth in. This simple and stylish accessory also makes a great gift.

Felt & Cut

Wool fabrics have different shrinking rates, so there's no way to predict the final measurements before felting the

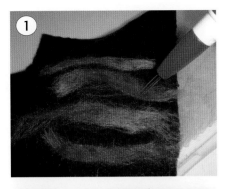

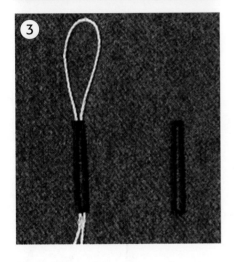

fabric. The neck warmer requires a 22"x43" wool rectangle, so 1 to 1½ yards of wool fabric is usually sufficient.

Machine wash and dry the fabric until the desired felted texture is achieved. The fabric may need to be washed and dried several times before the surface texture changes. Felting may not be evident until the fabric has been through the cycle eight times or more.

From the felted fabric, cut one 22"x43" rectangle. Adjust the rectangle size if desired. The width should fit loosely enough to be comfortable but snug enough to keep the neck warm.

Embellish

Using a chalk marker, draw vertical lines along one rectangle long edge, varying the line height and spacing to create an interesting design.

Place yarn or thin wisps of roving along each marked line, and then needle felt the yarn or roving in place. Add more yarn or roving layers as needed to achieve the desired look.

Construct

With wrong sides together, fold the rectangle in half lengthwise. Using a short zigzag or satin stitch, stitch the rectangle open edges. Felted wool doesn't ravel, so use a straight stitch if desired for a different look.

Using a chalk marker, draw a diagonal line for the buttonhole 2" from the rectangle upper-right corner. Draw the line length according to the button size.

If your machine has a corded buttonhole foot, refer to the manual to stitch the corded buttonhole. This creates a sturdy buttonhole that won't stretch with use.

To manually create a corded buttonhole, set the machine to a narrow satin stitch slightly wider than the cord width. Fold the cord in half, abutting the two cord lengths along the line. Stitch over each cord length along the buttonhole marking (**3**). Pull the cord free ends until the buttonhole is slightly puckered; clip the ends close to the stitching. Smooth the fabric so the cord disappears under the stitching, and then cut open the buttonhole.

Place the rectangle right end over the left end, and mark the desired button placement through the buttonhole. Hand stitch the button in place.

To wear the neck warmer, wrap it around your neck and button the ends. Fold the upper edges like a collar, or scrunch them downward like a cowl. Arrange the warmer with the button at the center front or to the side as desired. ✄

NEW
Boundaries

{ by Janis Bullis }

Create a one-of-a-kind throw using soft fleece and
pieced binding in colors that match your home décor.

Supplies

- 50" square of fleece
- 9 coordinating fat quarters (1 each of 3 colors and 2 each of 3 colors)
- All-purpose thread
- Removable fabric marker
- Rotary cutting system

Cut

From three fat quarters, cut twelve 1³/₄"x 22" strips. From three additional fat quarters, cut thirty-six 1¼"x 22" strips. From the remaining three fat quarters, cut thirty-six 1³/₄"x 22" strips.

Construct

Use ¼" seam allowances to piece the fat quarter strips.

With right sides together, align one wide strip with one narrow strip; stitch one long edge, and then press open the seam. Repeat to attach four additional strips, alternating strip widths **(1)**. Repeat to stitch 12 identical pieced panels.

Mark 7½" from one panel short edge, using a removable fabric marker. Mark 7½" from the first mark. Mark 7½" from the previous mark. Using a rotary cutter, mat and clear ruler, cut the panel at a 45° angle beginning at each mark **(2)**.

Discard the triangles and reserve the two parallelograms.

Repeat to cut the remaining 11 panels to yield 24 parallelograms.

With right sides together, align one parallelogram short edge; pin, and then stitch. Press open the seam **(3)**. Repeat to attach the remaining parallelograms to create one long binding strip.

Using a removable fabric marker, draw a line 1½" inside the fleece perimeter.

Bind

Use ½" seam allowances to attach the binding to the fleece.

Beginning at one fleece-edge center, position the binding long edge along the marked line with right sides together. Fold the binding beginning ½" toward the wrong side to conceal the raw edges. Stitch the binding lower edge to the fleece **(4)**.

To miter the corners, raise the needle, turn the fabric, and fold the binding up and back down over itself **(5)**. Lower the needle and continue to stitch the binding 1½" from the fleece edge.

Continue stitching the binding to the fleece, mitering each corner. When you reach the beginning of the binding, trim the binding end so it fits inside the beginning fold.

Wrap the binding around the fleece edge, folding each corner to miter. Slipstitch the binding fold to the fleece, and then slipstitch each mitered corner from the front and back side. ✂

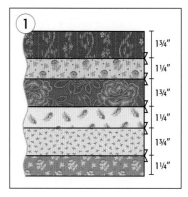

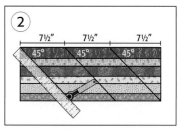

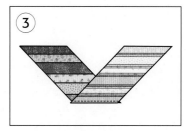

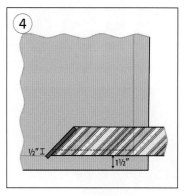

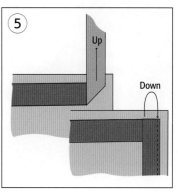

BINDING FUN

Use pieced binding to make other fun projects.

- Bind a quilt with the pieced binding. Use solid complementary colors or use the quilt fabric to make the binding.
- Use flannel to piece the binding for a softer feel that's perfect for a baby.
- Use several colors for the binding strips to add a personal touch. For example, use red, white and blue strips for a 4th of July theme. Or create a fun Christmas blanket using green, red and white. Or use the colors of the rainbow for a child.
- Bind a skirt lower edge using a narrow pieced binding strip.
- Add pizzazz to jacket sleeves by binding the sleeve openings with pieced binding.

A CUT
aBOVE

{ by Carol Zentgraf }

Wool felt doesn't fray, so it's ideal for reverse appliqué designs. Easily create a custom wool felt place mat design using stencils, stamps or photographs.

Supplies

Supplies listed are enough to create one 13"x18" place mat.

- 14"x19" rectangle each of two wool felt colors (See "Sources.")
- Two fusible web sheets (See "Sources.")
- Stencils, stamps or photographs for design
- Contrasting all-purpose or heavyweight thread (See "Sources.")
- Rotary cutter with decorative blade
- Sharp pointed scissors
- Fine-tip marker (optional)
- Fabric ink or acrylic paint (optional)
- Foam paintbrush (optional)

Prepare

When selecting a reverse appliqué design, keep in mind that designs with large cut-out areas are easier to work with than designs with intricate details. Choose from a variety of methods to create reverse appliqué designs, including stenciling, stamping and tracing **(1)**.

Designate one felt rectangle as the place mat upper layer and the remaining felt rectangle as the lower layer.

Align two fusible web sheets over the upper-layer wrong side; fuse, following the manufacturer's instructions **(2)**. Fuse the web sheets before applying the design to the backing to avoid shifting the design placement.

Stencil

Because stencils are a continuous design, they're ideal to use for reverse appliqué designs. Choose stencil designs in proportionate sizes for the project. Combine designs from two or more stencils, if desired.

Trace the chosen stencil outline onto the fusible web backing **(3)**. Keep in mind that the design will be reversed on the place mat right side when the design is cut out and that the place mat edges will be trimmed ¼".

Stamp

Use large stamps designed for fabric or home décor projects. Clear stamps are especially useful in ensuring exact design placement.

Use a foam paintbrush to apply a thin coat of acrylic paint to the stamp or press the stamp onto an ink pad. Press the stamp straight down onto the fusible web paper backing and lift it straight up. Repeat as desired **(4)**.

Photograph

Use photographs of objects that have clearly defined outlines as a basis for the design. Upload the photograph into the computer. Enlarge or reduce the design size as desired using image-editing software; print.

Trace the design onto the fusible web before fusing the web to the felt. Place the fusible web over the image with the paper backing facing up. If needed, outline the design on

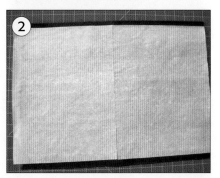

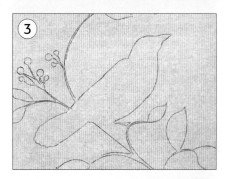

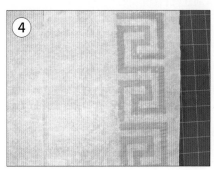

Tip: If using a design with multiple elements, copy a portion of the design to use as an accent on the opposite corner.

the photograph using a dark marker to aid in tracing through the fusible web. Use a fine-tip permanent marker to trace the desired element outline onto the paper backing (5).

Fuse the web sheets to the felt.

Construct

If applying the design after fusing, allow the backing to cool, and then apply the design to the backing using the desired method.

Using sharp pointed scissors, make a small snip within the design. Cut out the designs. If the chosen design is large with long lines or gradual curves, use an 18mm or 25mm rotary cutter, and then cut the smaller details using sharp pointed scissors (6).

Remove the paper backing and place the rectangle right side up over the place mat lower layer, aligning the edges. Press with steam to fuse the layers.

Edgestitch the design perimeters using contrasting thread. Use heavyweight thread for more prominent stitching.

Position the place mat on a cutting mat and mark ¼" inside the perimeter using a removable fabric marker. Use a rotary cutter with a decorative blade to cut along the lines. Or trim the edges using pinking shears or scissors that have decorative blades.

Topstitch the place mat perimeter using a ½" seam allowance and the same thread color used to edgestitch the design. ✄

SOURCES

Coats & Clark provided the heavyweight thread: (800) 648-1479, coatsandclark.com.

National Nonwovens provided the wool felt: (800) 333-3469, nationalnonwovens.com.

The Warm Company provided the Steam-A-Seam 2 fusible web sheets: (425) 248-2424, warmcompany.com.

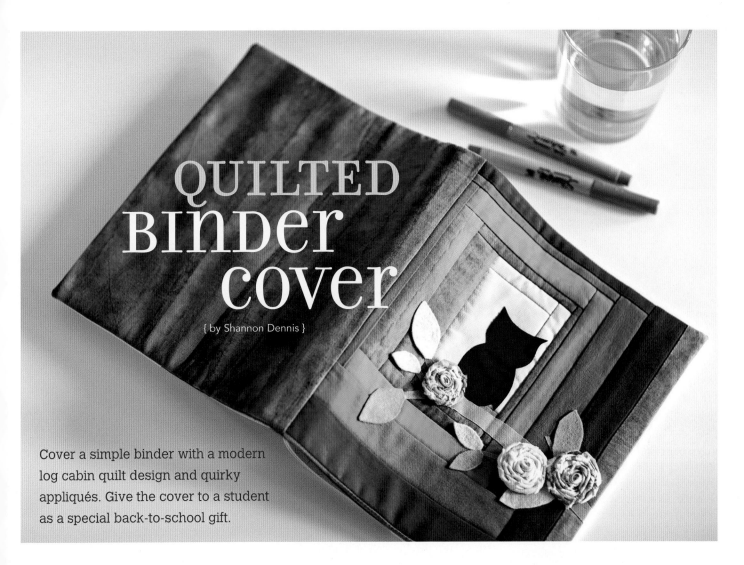

QUILTED binder cover

{ by Shannon Dennis }

Cover a simple binder with a modern log cabin quilt design and quirky appliqués. Give the cover to a student as a special back-to-school gift.

Supplies

- **4 to 6 coordinating blue fabric scraps (amount determined by binder size)**
- **Muslin, print cotton, solid cotton & fusible fleece (exact amount determined by binder size)**
- **3" square of brown fabric**
- **4"x6" rectangle of light brown fabric**
- **Scrap of green felt & print cotton fabric**
- **6"x8" rectangle of fusible web**
- **Removable fabric marker**
- **Hand sewing needle**
- **Fabric glue**

TIP: Embellish the cover with beads, buttons, fabric flowers or other charms for a personalized look.

Prepare

Open the binder and place it on a flat work surface with the wrong side facing down. Measure the length; add 1", and then record. Measure the height; add 1", and then record.

From the muslin and fusible fleece, cut one rectangle each according to the measurements. Adhere the fusible fleece to the muslin rectangle, following the manufacturer's instructions. Designate the muslin as the cover right side.

From the print cotton, cut one rectangle according to the recorded measurements for the lining. Cut one rectangle according to the height and recorded length divided in half for the back cover.

From the solid cotton, cut two rectangles measuring 8"x the height measurement for the flaps.

Cut each blue fabric scrap into a strip measuring 1"- to 2"-wide and as long as possible.

From the lightest blue fabric scrap, cut one 2½"x3½" rectangle for the log cabin center. Designate one rectangle short edge as the upper edge.

Construct

Use ½" seam allowances unless otherwise noted.

Fold the cover in half widthwise with wrong sides together; press, and then unfold. Position the cover right side up on a flat work surface. Mark the cover centerline. Designate one cover long edge as the upper edge and the cover right half as the front.

Mark the desired log cabin design center on the front. Center the log cabin rectangle right side up over the

mark with the upper edge parallel to the cover upper edge; baste the perimeter.

With right sides together, stitch one light blue strip to the center rectangle upper edge using a scant ¼" seam allowance and stitching through all layers **(1)**. Press the strip upward and trim the excess fabric to align with the center rectangle edges.

Repeat to stitch another light blue strip to the rectangle right edge and previous strip right edge **(2)**. Press the strip upward and trim the excess fabric to align with the rectangle and previous strip edges.

Repeat to stitch additional strips around the rectangle perimeter, graduating the strip colors from lightest to darkest and alternating strip widths as desired until the front cover is filled slightly beyond the perimeter. Remove the rectangle basting stitches.

Mark the cover centerline. With right sides together, position the back cover over the front cover, aligning the raw edges; pin. Stitch along the centerline using a ¼" seam allowance **(3)**. Fold the back cover right side up; press.

Fold each flap in half lengthwise with wrong sides together; press. Designate one flap short edge as the upper edge. Position the lining rectangle right side

up on a flat work surface. Designate one rectangle long edge as the upper edge. Position one flap over the lining, aligning the upper and right side edges; baste the flap raw edges. Baste the remaining flap over the lining left edge **(4)**.

With right sides together, stitch the cover and lining perimeter, leaving a 4" opening along the lower edge for turning. Trim the corners and grade the seams. Turn the cover right side out through the opening; press. Slipstitch the opening closed.

Embellish

Trace the owl, branch and leaf templates on page 63.

Adhere fusible web to the brown square, light brown rectangle and felt scrap wrong side following the manufacturer's instructions. Trace each appliqué outline onto the corresponding fabric fusible paper backing. Cut out each appliqué.

Position the appliqués on the front cover, referring to the image at left; fuse.

From print cotton fabric scraps, cut three 1"x10" strips. Tightly twist each fabric strip and wind into a small rosette. Adhere the rosettes to the front cover using fabric glue.

Insert the binder into the cover. ❧

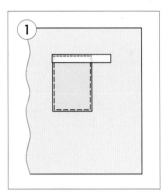

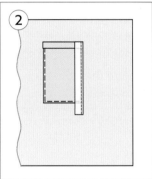

Centerline

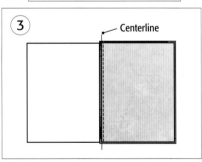

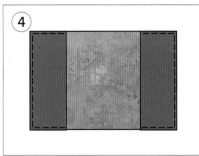

Quilted Binder Cover
Owl, Leaf & Branch Templates

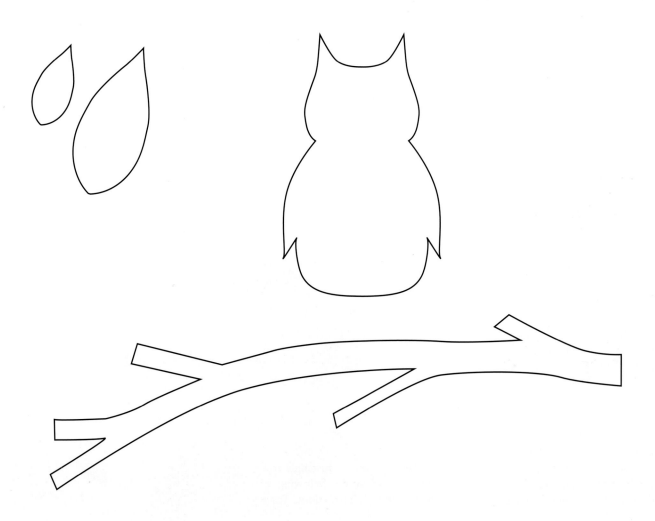

Flag Template

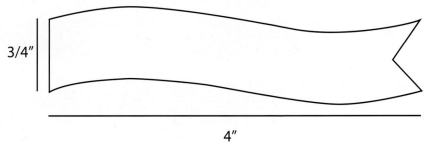

3/4"

4"

COOL TOOLS FOR EXCELLENT embellishments

Have fun personalizing your projects with cool embellishments, ranging from beads and sequins to foiling and hot-fix crystals.

Fabric dye is a quick and easy way to transform fabric. Acid dyes work best with protein fibers, such as wool, silk or fur. Fiber reactive dyes are best for cotton, rayon and linen. Disperse dye is perfect for polyester and nylon (A).

Fabric paint is available in sprays, pens and liquids, and work best on natural fibers, such as cotton. Prewash garments and test-paint on scrap fabric to ensure desired results (B).

Fabric discharging is the technique of removing dye using bleach in certain areas, resulting in an interesting textured look. Bleach gel pens are great for creating tidy discharge designs on colored fabric. Or try a cleaning gel with bleach on rubber stamps to produce interesting designs (C).

Beads and sequins add special flair to garments, bags and home décor items. Vary the color combinations and patterns for a truly exceptional look (D).

Grommets are metal or plastic rings that are inserted into fabric holes for reinforcement or fastening. Grommets can also serve as decorative elements in garments or purses (E).

Hot-fix crystals and metals add pizzaz to home-dec projects, garments, costumes and accessories (F).

Hot-fix application tool includes special tips that make attaching hot-fix crystals, pearls and metals effortless (G).

Foiling adds sparkle and flair to fabric. Some foiling sheets must be adhered using an iron, while others are ready to go after rubbing. Foiling is washable, and the sheets can be used until all the color wears off (H).

Patches are embroidered, printed or embellished fabric cutout designs that can be sewn or ironed onto fabric. Use ready-made patches to embellish bags or clothing, or make your own patches using appliqué embroidery designs (I).

Transfers are special images or letters that permanently fuse to cotton, linen or rayon using an iron. Purchase premade image transfers individually or in kits, or purchase transfer paper to create unique transfers using pictures on a home computer (J).

SOURCES

Creative Crystal provided the BeJeweler Pro Electric Rhinestone Setter and hot-fix crystals, metals and pearls: (800) 578-0716, creativecrystal.com.

DMC Creative World provided the Say It with Stitches Iron-On Alphabet Transfers: www.dmc-usa.com.

Embellishment Village provided the foiling sheets, foiling glue and stencils: (877) 639-9820, embellishmentvillage.com.

Glitz! Hot-Fix Crystals provided the hot-fix crystals, metals and pearls: (865) 357-2541, hotfixcrystals.com.

Madison Art Shop carries the Shiva Professional Paintstiks: (800) 284-4846; madisonartshop.com.

Michael's carries the Tulip fabric dye and fabric paint: (800) 642-4235, michaels.com.

Prym Consumer USA, Inc. provided the grommets: dritz.com.

Rit Dye provided the powder fabric dye: (866) 794-0800, ritdye.com.

Simply Spray provided the soft fabric paint: simplyspray.com.